MARGARET JONAS was .... Steiner House, London, for many years, and has studied anthroposophy since 1974. Her special interests include history, religion, astrology, astronomy, literature, the Grail, psychology and states of consciousness. She has been researching the Knights Templar for more than 30 years, and is the editor of an anthology by Rudolf Steiner on the subject. She has edited several other anthologies of Steiner's work and has written articles for various journals. She lives in Sussex, England, and has one son.

THE TEMPLAR SPIRIT

*The Esoteric Inspiration, Rituals and Beliefs
of the Knights Templar*

Margaret Jonas

TEMPLE LODGE

Temple Lodge Publishing
Hillside House, The Square
Forest Row, RH18 5ES

www.templelodge.com

Published by Temple Lodge 2011

A catalogue record for this book is available from the British Library

ISBN 978 1 906999 25 4

Cover by Andrew Morgan Design
Typeset by DP Photosetting, Neath, West Glamorgan
Printed and bound by Gutenberg Press, Malta

MIX
Paper from
responsible sources
FSC
www.fsc.org   FSC® C022612

Contents

Acknowledgements

I should like to thank the Humanities Section of the School of Spiritual Science for its generous grant towards the publication of this book, and also Juliet Faith for supplying a photo of the Cameley head.

Part One

THE INSPIRERS

Introduction

This work assumes a basic familiarity with the history and downfall of the Order of Knights Templar (1118–1314), founded ostensibly to protect pilgrims travelling to Jerusalem but having much wider and deeper purposes for both medieval life and future Christian development. For more background, readers are directed to general histories and to the author's compilation of material from Rudolf Steiner, published as *The Knights Templar*,[1] whose spiritual-scientific research and insights have inspired these studies. It may seem strange that the three things the Templars are best known for—their courage and prowess in battle, their banking and financial institutions and their ideals for brotherhood and community life—are barely touched upon in these pages. Instead we are looking at an aspect of Templar history which is least known about, but which at the same time has accumulated the most wild speculations: the Templars' spiritual or esoteric life and practices.

Non nobis, Domine, non nobis, sed Nomini Tuo da Gloriam (Not for us, Lord, not for us, but in Thy Name the Glory) sums up the Templars' ideal. They strove to live up to this ideal in such a way that '... The blood of the Templar belonged to Christ Jesus—each one of them knew this ... Every moment of their life was to be filled with the perpetual consciousness of how in their own soul there dwelt—in the words of St Paul—"not I, but Christ in me"'.[2] This must surely be underpinned by a strong and active religious life. When not in battle situations they were required to live the life of other monastic orders. Having taken the three vows of poverty, chastity and obedience, they would say the regular daily Offices, pray and hear Mass whenever possible.

The Templars' rise to becoming a successful elite community was remarkable, but so too was their falling prey to machinations and being so spectacularly slandered and destroyed—which suggests that they were indeed in possession of something even deeper than most medieval religious practices. This has been misunderstood, however, and interpreted as their having material wealth in the form of special 'treasure', mysterious ancient artefacts bestowing special powers, the Holy Grail, a bloodline of Christ, and so on. Behind all religious life are the deeper powers which lead to *initiation*, i.e. knowledge, experience and understanding of the spiritual world which opens up to the pupil on the path, though it may be experienced in a less structured form ('...their souls were so inspired by intense devotion to the Christian impulse and the Mystery of Golgotha that consequently many knights experienced a Christian initiation').[3] Rudolf Steiner has described in various places a sevenfold path of initiation followed in earlier times, which he calls the Christian-Gnostic. It involves strongly meditating upon the stages of Christ's Passion as described in St John's Gospel:

> The guidance concerning initiation is of the highest authority, that of Jesus Christ. John's Gospel gives such guidance. It is not a book for study but a book for life in the true sense of the word ... the images of the Gospel will gradually slip quietly into our dreams, so that we have real inner experience of the events described ...
>
> ...a symbolic act in which one humbly confesses one's dependence and the fact that one has grown and developed on the basis of something lower, at a lower level than our own, certain symptoms will show themselves also externally—a strange feeling of water running by one's feet ... an imaginative vision of the washing of the feet ... marks the first stage.
>
> The second station is the scourging... It means that in spite of the great and frequent pain and troubles we have to bear in life we will always stand up straight and not grow faint-hearted. Again we have both outer and inner symptoms—a strange physical stabbing sensation and the mental image of our own scourging.
>
> Stage three is the crown of thorns. This means that though it is painful to have our most sacred feelings and convictions derided and have scorn poured on them, we must not lose our

inner firmness, our equilibrium. Symptoms are headaches, and vision of one's own person wearing the crown of thorns. Fourthly bearing the cross (crucifixion). Here the pupil is to gain living experience that the body is really an indifferent object compared to the soul ... and we'll truly control it. Symptoms are Christ's stigmata appearing as reddened areas on hands and feet. This blood trial only occurs for brief moments during the meditation however. Inner vision of being crucified oneself.

Fifth, the mystic death ... It is as if the whole world around him is covered by a veil. When he feels himself thus to be in utter darkness, the veil will suddenly tear and he looks through it into a new, wondrous world ... This mystic death is like a descent into hell.

The pupil is now someone who has been awakened and can progress to the sixth stage, the entombment. Here he feels the whole outer environment to be his body ... The body feels itself to be one with the earth, and individual consciousness expands to become earth consciousness.

The seventh stage cannot be described to any degree, for it is beyond all powers of imagination based on the senses ... This stage involves entering into perfect divinity and glory, and we do not have the words to describe it.[4]

Today it has become more difficult to follow such a mystical path. Whether the knights would have consciously followed it is hard to say—literacy was not common to all. They would have doubtless received oral and pictorial guidance, and perhaps some of them practised at least part of it and were able to achieve a certain level of initiation.

In addition the Templars appear to have had their own teachings about which we know very little. An attempt to penetrate something of this controversial area is to be found in the second part of this book.

The first part came about as a result of the question: who might have been the inspiring human beings behind the Order? Accepting the inspiration of *spiritual* beings is assumed, but it seems relevant to ask which historical figures might have lent their wisdom and guidance to the founding of the Order? It may be asked why St Bernard of Clairvaux is not included here, apart from within the Grail chapter. St Bernard greatly inspired the Order by giving them their Rule at the command of the Pope in 1128 or 1129, ten years after the founding of the Order. He was the nephew of André de Montbard, one of the founding knights, and he also wrote *In Praise of the New Knighthood* at the request of Hughes de Payens, which to our ears sounds uncomfortably 'crusading'. The inclusion of an extract in James Wasserman's book *The Templars and the Assassins*[5] shows how the modern mind quickly equates such 'ideals' these days with Islamic Jihad. St Bernard had intended to become a knight himself but experienced a religious conversion and joined the Cistercian Order, becoming the Abbot of Clairvaux aged 25. He combined mystical wisdom and insight with practical organizing skills and did much to create a *practical* way of life, which united the ideals of monasticism and knighthood. But it is open to question whether he would be one of the original inspirers, who were initiated individualities of the highest standing.

1. St John the Baptist

The Order of the Knights Templar wanted to found a sun view of Christianity, a view of Christianity that looked up again to Christ as a sun Being, as a cosmic Being, a view that knew again about the spirits of the planets and stars...[6]

It is often said that the Templars belonged to the 'Johannine' stream of Christianity, meaning one that is more esoteric than the 'Petrine' or church Christianity.[7] Generally people assume that John the Evangelist, the beloved disciple, is meant by this as the leading inspirer, but it is in fact the Baptist who is really meant by this designation. Such is the reverence extended to him by some sources that it is sometimes even assumed that Jesus was not meant to surpass him—that John was perhaps the true Messiah.[8] Following the Baptism as described by St John in the Bible, the Baptist speaks the well-known words 'He must increase, and I must decrease' (John 3:30), so it is clear that he himself was making no such claim. However, St John's Day, 24 June, the said birth of the Baptist, was honoured by the Templars and subsequently by Freemasons. It is highly unlikely that either of these orders could have known the series of incarnations of the Baptist as revealed by Rudolf Steiner, except perhaps of Elijah as this possibility is mentioned in the Gospels.[9] Steiner revealed that subsequently John reappeared as the Renaissance artist Raphael and later as the eighteenth-century German poet Novalis (Friedrich von Hardenberg).[10] These two, of course, are not relevant to the age of the Templars as such, but more importantly indicate that this individuality has a *future task,* a fact which was apparently known in the higher echelons of the Order. His purpose was to prepare humanity for the Christian 'baptism of fire'—the receiving of the Holy Spirit, which first manifested at Pentecost—at a time when true Christianity and brother-sisterhood would be understood, not in the twelfth or thirteenth centuries or even in the present age, but in the future sixth post-Atlantean epoch, the age not of Pisces but of Aquarius, which begins in the year 2375. John represents the Water Carrier—the sign of Aquarius, a constellation associated traditionally with the ideal of a future harmonious community of universal brother and sisterhood based on spiritually evolved values.

> It was made clear [...] that Christianity, which began as a seed, would in future bear something quite different as fruit, and that by the name Water Carrier was meant John [the Baptist] who scatters Christianity as a seed [...] Aquarius or the Water Carrier points to the same person as John who baptizes with water in order to prepare mankind to receive the Christian baptism of fire. The fact of the coming of a 'John/ Aquarius' who will first confirm the old John and announce a new Christ who will renew the temple [...] this was taught in the depths of the Templar Mysteries, so that the event should be understood.[11]

John was thus their forerunner: '[The Templars] said "Christ as represented by the western Church means nothing to us. But we proclaim the Christ who walked in Jerusalem and received initiation through the Baptist; therefore our teachers about Christ are not the teachers and fathers of the Church but John, the initiator himself is our teacher." '[12] 'Renewing the temple' is akin to creating a new community—one of the Templar ideals was to bring harmony to the three principal faiths of Christianity, Judaism and Islam, especially in the Holy Land.

The glyph for Aquarius is ♒ two waves. But are the waves really pertaining to water? It is more likely that they refer to living, etheric forces (life forces), often denoted as 'water' in esoteric language, though readers familiar with astrology will be aware of Aquarius as an 'air' sign. (The origin of this allocation of the four elements to the zodiac is hard to trace, and seems to have more to do with the moon's influence on life forces and plant life.) In this 'water' we can experience the soul or psychic energy in our thought and feeling life. The following post-Atlantean epoch is the sixth, the age of Aquarius, 2375–4535, based on the constellation rising at the spring equinox. The cultural age of Aquarius begins later, 3574–5734,[13] which is when the transformation of consciousness really takes hold and the new culture will be flowering, the age of brother- and sisterhood when people understand this flow of energy between one another, when empathy is so developed that a person actually cannot be happy if someone else is suffering.

The rite of baptism as total immersion in water comes from Jewish purification rites, especially those that were more esoteric, as practised by the Essenes,[14] for until Jesus came to him by the River Jordan, John was not performing 'Christian' baptisms. They were intended to bring about not only a ritual purification but an inner transformation and were accompanied by other forms of spiritual training. Steiner has described how in these older rites total immersion would have resulted in a loosening of the etheric body from the physical, thus allowing spiritual forces to enter the soul of the one being baptized who all the while was being protected from an absolute disconnection of the etheric body and death by the strength of the initiator. With respect to Jesus himself, it was the moment at which the Christ Being entered him. The 'Son of Man' or perfected human being became the 'Son of God'. By the time of Christ the initiatory loosening effect was becoming less and less possible as physical and etheric bodies became more closely wedded. Nonetheless, immersion had a significant effect upon the soul life. Even if the subtle bodies no longer separated, people could still experience their 'life tableau', which can still happen in near-death experiences, especially drowning. Immersion—without the baptized being held under the water for any length of time—still continues in certain Christian Churches, though total immersion was deemed 'unnecessary' by the Council of Ravenna in 1311. It is possible that a deeper understanding of baptism had been lost by this time. The date is close to the demise of the Templar Order, an interesting synchronicity. Adult baptism addresses the human spirit, the true ego, which can incorporate Christ, whereas baptism for infants is more a sacramental act of receiving them into a community of Christians—though a valid act, one cannot help feeling that something has been lost or weakened thereby.

We can get some idea of the pre-Christian significance around the time of John by considering the still surviving sect of the Mandaeans. A curious survival from earlier times, these Gnostic believers are today found mainly in Iraq (although they are now having to seek refuge in Syria and Jordan due to persecution by extremist Muslims). They practise baptism and revere John the Baptist or 'Yahjah', and are thought to possess secret rites and knowledge which they guard carefully from outsiders. Their 'Great Book' (*sidra rba*) also known as the 'Treasure' (*ginza*) and 'Book of John' (*drasa d-yahya* or *-yuhana*) are compilations for the ascent of the soul. Though sometimes considered as Muslim, their writings pre-date Islam and demonstrate the early Gnostic tradition which was found especially in Syria. They teach of a world of light located in the north, opposed by a world of darkness in the south. The ruler of darkness is limited when a messenger of light, the 'Gnosis of Life', *manda d'haiya*, puts him in fetters. They rejected Christianity yet show some features of Manichaean ideas. Their custom of baptizing by immersion in flowing or 'living' water which they call 'Jordan' shows their descent from the Baptist's mission. Although now in Iraq they originated from the Jews and would have been still extant in the Holy Land in the Middle Ages. Because of their secrecy, whether contact was made with Templars is uncertain. Andrew Welburn, in the best description of Mandaean beliefs, considers that their practices go back even earlier, to the Mystery rites of ancient Babylon. The initiated Mandaean would be raised up to a new life through baptism and called a 'king'. In Babylonian beliefs the god Ea, or wisdom, guarded the springs of living water which welled up from the divine origin, or abyss.[15] Ea was sometimes called 'the god with streams' and was depicted holding a pot or with water streaming from his arms. He later came to be associated with the constellation of Aquarius (but also with Capricorn).[16] The consciousness of 'living water' and its significance would have been meaningful also to the Baptist. The feeling for a god of the waters continued down to the time of the Renaissance when artists often depicted a river spirit in the Jordan whilst the Baptism takes place. In this mosaic from St Mark's, Venice, the river god is shown (bottom, to right) and also three angelic beings.

The Baptism. Basilica di S. Marco, Venice

Returning to the being of John himself, we learn from Steiner that he was a vessel through which an angel could work[17] (a possibility for an advanced soul), an angel from the sphere of the moon. Sometimes John is even depicted with wings.

Sergei Prokofieff makes the suggestion, based on Steiner's insights, that this angel of John's was the one who had formerly been the guardian angel of the Buddha, and on the Buddha's ascent to the angelic level had then risen to the rank of archangel but continued to work as an angel. In this capacity he is known to us under the name Vidar, the Norse god who was the son of Odin.[18] He survives Ragnarok—the 'Twilight of the Gods'—and overcomes the Fenris Wolf, an ahrimanic entity. This angel working through John was, according to Steiner, working from the moon sphere, which is the home of beings involved in visionary clairvoyance (and also of mighty beings of wisdom).[19] The Fenris Wolf is an entity who perpetrates a false, misleading

*John the Baptist. Fifteenth
century Byzantine icon.
Galleria dell'Accademia,
Florence*

kind of clairvoyance and attempts to obscure the presence of
Christ from spiritual sight in the etheric.[20] In spiritual science, the
'Moon' stage of evolution was when 'water' was created. Thus
John is the Water Bearer or Aquarius initiate, there being twelve
sacred mysteries of the sun in the zodiac—experiences that go far
deeper than any superficial 'sun sign' astrology. John protects
true 'living' water or life forces from 'pollution' by adversary
forces and is a helper in distinguishing true clairvoyance from
false. Steiner speaks about the Aquarius initiation in this way:

> John the Baptist had necessarily to receive an Aquarius
> Initiation, the expression indicating that the sun was standing
> in the constellation of Aquarius. Try to understand it in this
> way. On the day or light side of the zodiac lie Aries, Taurus,
> Gemini, Cancer, Leo, Virgo, then Libra. The constellations on
> the night or dark side of the zodiac are Scorpio, Sagittarius,
> Capricorn, Aquarius and Pisces. Since the last two lie on the
> night side, the sun's rays coming from them must not only

traverse physical space but they must send the spiritual light of
the sun, which passes *through* the earth, through spiritual
space. Aquarius initiates received this name because they were
able to confer the water-baptism, that is to say, to enable
human beings, while immersed in water, to be sustained by the
power of the spiritual sun. [...] If we trace the course of the
sun in the heavens we find that as the physical sun sets the
spiritual sun begins to rise. In its day or summer course the
sun progresses from Taurus to Aries, and so on; in its night or
winter course it will reveal to us the secrets of the initiation of
Aquarius or Pisces. Physically, the sun's course is from Virgo
to Leo, Cancer, Gemini, Taurus, Aries: spiritually its course is
from Virgo to Libra, Scorpio, Sagittarius, Capricorn and
Aquarius to Pisces. The spiritual counterpart of the course of
the physical sun is its passage from Aquarius to Pisces.[21]

These words are very puzzling, what can Steiner mean here? Is
there a mistake in the transcript? Steiner has spoken very little of
the 'day' and 'night' side . The 'day' half would be those constellations belonging to the longer daylight hours, from Aries
through to Libra. The 'night' ones would be those of the darker,
winter months. Even though every day throughout the year all
twelve rise and set, day or night (except for the far northerly and
southerly regions of the earth), they still have something of the
quality of 'day' and 'night' about them irrespective of these
rhythms. My understanding of the above passage is as follows:
'as the physical sun sets, the spiritual sun begins to rise'—if the
sun is setting in Pisces, for example, Virgo is rising above the
horizon in the east. Aquarius would have already set. When the
sun is on the other side of the earth, its spiritual power works
through the earth.

'Physically the sun's course is from Virgo to Leo, Cancer...' I
think Steiner is using 'the sun's course' as a term to mean the
daily movement of the zodiac constellations across the sky, rising from east to west. All twelve rise and set in 24 hours, taking
approximately two hours each (some in fact have a shorter time
of ascension and others longer depending on latitude and the

obliquity of the earth's axis). If we look at them in the heavens
from the earth, facing south and 'reading' as we do from left to
right, we will see them apparently moving across in the order
that appears the *reverse* of the sun's monthly course, i.e. Virgo
(just rising), Leo, Cancer, Gemini, Taurus, Aries, Pisces just
setting; if we can see them in the night sky at such a moment, our
vision would be of a reversed order across the sky. Whilst these
constellations are glittering in the heavens, the *spiritual* forces of
the sun are passing through the earth and can be perceived by
initiate consciousness.

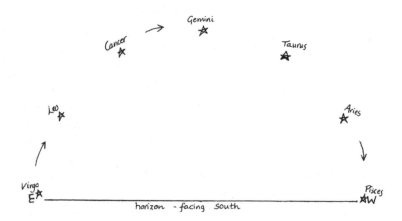

'Spiritually its course is from Virgo to Libra, Scorpio ...' Whilst
the first group has risen above the horizon, this group is working
spiritually from below the earth. At the same time, the *monthly*
course of the sun would be from Aries to Taurus, Gemini,
Cancer, etc.

> Consequently John could say: He must increase but I must
> decrease. My mission is one of which you will have a picture
> when the Sun passes from the sign of Aquarius to that of
> Pisces. I am an Aquarius Initiate and I am not worthy to give
> you the secrets of the Sun in Pisces. I am not worthy to
> unloose the shoe-latchet of the One I am to proclaim to you.[21]

When Aquarius has set, Pisces is still just above the horizon, about to set. Thus we need to understand three kinds of zodiacal movement:

1. The daily rhythm from east to west, in which the signs appear in reverse order.
2. The monthly passage of the sun from sign to sign—the sun being active during the night as well as during the day with its spiritual forces passing through the earth.
3. The precession of the equinox whereby the sun rises in spring in each constellation of the zodiacal epochs, based on the sign rising at the spring equinox, are also in reverse order. The age of Aquarius will *follow* that of Pisces. John precedes Christ (Aquarius precedes Pisces in the daily rhythm), but the Aquarian age he was preparing for will follow that of the Piscean.

The power of the sun was present all the time in Christ during the three years he lived and worked on the earth in a human body. The spiritual sun worked through him so that he is described as performing healings after the sun had set or before sunrise. Night-time consciousness is the time of initiation knowledge—Nicodemus came to Christ 'by night'. It was perhaps not just for reasons of secrecy that it is said that the chapters of the Templars' inner order were held at night. It is probably no coincidence that Novalis, the later incarnation of John, wrote poems entitled *Hymns to the Night*, in which he describes being led to the soul of his deceased fiancée Sophie, and then on to experience the spiritual being of wisdom—Sophia.

John the Baptist's emblem is the *Agnus Dei*, Lamb of God, or the 'lamb and flag', the lamb being an ancient symbol of Christ's sacrificial deed: 'Behold the lamb of God which taketh away the sin of the world' (John 1:29), John's words at the Baptism, and the flag or banner is said to be an emblem of victory or truce. This emblem was used by several Templar masters as their personal seal. The master or preceptor was in charge of a local commanderie or preceptory and would be involved in signing documents such as for the transfer or sale of land, or for overseeing truces. Examples of its use were the seals of a master in Provence, Roncelin de Fos, and masters of the English Temple, Richard of Hastings, Robert de Samfort (or Sanford), and William de la More. Now it is the emblem for the 'Middle Temple' inns of court in London's Strand, the site of the former Templar preceptory. We might wish that an Aquarius-inspired 'baptism' or initiation might still flow out from those ancient portals into the hectic life of today and guide people towards future spiritual goals.

2. St John the Evangelist

This St John is commonly taken to be the author of the fourth Gospel and the Book of Revelation. Conventional scholarship assumes him to have been John Zebedee, brother of James, but Rudolf Steiner's research reveals otherwise. He describes the miracle of the Raising of Lazarus and how this was in fact an older form of initiation which had become too dangerous and Lazarus may have actually almost died. It was, however, also the first Christian initiation and Lazarus took the name John thereafter.[23] He becomes 'the disciple whom Jesus loved'. When we read in the scriptures that Christ Jesus 'loved' someone, it was not merely an expression of feeling, but of initiation power. In Rudolf Steiner's very last lecture to the Anthroposophical Society members,[24] he reveals why Lazarus took this name: the being of John the Baptist (who had by now been put to death by King Herod Antipas) had entered into him and was apparently for the remaining incarnation united with him. Steiner was too ill to conclude his exposition, but the mystery has been elaborated in more detail by various authors (see Hella Wiesberger, Sergei Prokofieff, Karl König, Edward Reaugh Smith and others,[25] all of whom shed valuable light on it). We are to understand that in subsequent incarnations the two individualities followed more independent destinies again.

We have mentioned John the Baptist's reappearance as Raphael and Novalis, but what of John the Evangelist? We are told that he reincarnated in the Middle Ages as Christian Rosenkreutz, the founder of the Rosicrucian Brotherhood, and later in the eighteenth century as the Count of Saint-Germain. The story of Christian Rosenkreutz's two medieval appearances is a complex one and the reader is referred to Steiner's lectures *Esoteric Christianity*[26] where it is described. 'John' becomes a guiding figure within esoteric Christianity and a leading Master of the West.[27] Prior to his life as Lazarus-John he was also significant: he was the master builder of King Solomon's Temple, Hiram Abiff. A number of Masonic rituals involve the story of the murder and raising of Hiram. As the Scottish Rite especially is said to descend from the Templars who were not persecuted in Scotland, it is clear that there was knowledge at some level of the significance of the raising of *Lazarus*. The origins of Freemasonry from within Templarism are disputed by many historians, but firmly attested to by a number of branches of Masonry. The difficulty is that many orders and brotherhoods invent detailed 'genealogies' involving historical figures who are in no position to refute them, such as for instance, in recent times, the Priory of Sion—even a casual internet search will reveal many more.

The *Temple Legend* material played an important part in Steiner's early ritual Lodge work, the Misraim Service (*Misraim Dienst*), within the rite of Memphis-Misraim[28]—the 'temple' being an image of the perfected human being and of the future evolved human community. We cannot therefore imagine that 'John' was not also an inspiring being and guide to the Templars. Steiner has referred to the 'star wisdom' of the Templars, which has not come down to us, but Manfred Schmidt-Brabant describes the change of heart by the Queen of Sheba when she switched her affections from Solomon to Hiram as representing a shift of this wisdom into the stream of Cain,[29] the earlier incarnation of Hiram, the people of Sheba (Saba) being known for their star knowledge. During the historical period of the Templars on earth, the young man who was to become Christian Rosenkreutz was being prepared for his future mission when he would be reborn. There are suggestions that his identity was known to certain of the Cathars, even that he was saved from destruction at Montségur, and it is therefore possible that this was known to some of the Templars also, though at present this remains in the realm of hypothesis.[30]

Steiner gave further indications as to the 'John' incarnations, beginning with Cain, the son of Adam and Eve, and including the individuality behind the medieval legend of Flor and his beloved Blancheflor,[31] and subsequent to the Count of Saint-Germain as someone not known to outer history spanning the late nineteenth and early twentieth centuries.[32] The Rosicrucian

Master is the most famous after 'John', and Steiner speaks of the Rosicrucians as continuing the stream of Templar esotericism— although the initiation of Christian Rosenkreutz as described in *The Chymical Wedding* took a different form.

Concerning the legend of Flor and Blancheflor (or Flos and Blankflos in Conrad Fleck's version), Steiner speaks of this as a legend of Provence belonging to the initiation of the Grail knights and of the Templars.[33] The pair, born at the same time on the same day, grow up together and love one another dearly. At maturity they are separated and Flor undertakes a quest, a series of adventures to find Blancheflor. She is about to be married to a foreign ruler when Flor finds her, but the ruler's heart is eventually moved by the love of the pair and sets them free to marry and return to their homeland. In the legend they were also the grandparents of Charlemagne:

> But those who studied the legend more deeply, saw in Charles the Great the figure who, in a certain sense, united esoteric and exoteric Christianity ... in Flor and Blancheflor lived the rose and the lily—typifying souls who were to preserve in its purity the esoteric Christianity which had been taught by Dionysius the Areopagite and others. The rose—Flor or Flos—symbolized the human soul who has received the impulse of the ego, of personality, who lets the spiritual work out of his individuality, who has brought the ego-force down into the red blood. But the lily was the symbol of the soul who can only remain spiritual when the ego remains *outside...* Flor and Blancheflor symbolize the finding of the World Soul, the World Ego, the human soul or the human ego.[34]

It is hard to imagine this moving love story finding sympathy with the celibate Templars, reminding them of their renunciation of human joy in another. But if indeed it was told to them, it must have been in such a way as to emphasize the spiritual quest of man (or woman) for the higher self. The red and the white are of course important alchemical images for stages in the great work. And as in the Grail story with Feirefis and Repanse de Schoie, there is the theme of bringing together another faith with

Christianity—Blancheflor is Christian but not so Flor until he later converts.

The theme of uniting the ego and soul is continued in the story of the *Chymical Wedding* with the death, resurrection and marriage of the King and Queen, to which Brother Rosenkreutz is invited:

> This day, this day, this, this
> The Royal wedding is.
> Art thou thereto by Birth inclin'd,
> And unto joy of God design'd...[35]

In the story he does not undergo a love experience himself (he is 81), but he does experience the temptation of the Lady Venus underground on the fifth day. His whole emphasis is, however, on love in a wider sense as his attitude to the other wedding guests shows. St John's last words were said to have been, 'Children, love one another'.

3. The Master Jesus

It is difficult for conventional Christian belief or scholarship to accept Rudolf Steiner's findings concerning the mystery of the births of *two* Jesus children as described in St Matthew and St Luke's Gospels, with their distinctly different genealogies.[36] To go further into this mystery would take us too far from the Templars, but there is considerable evidence that some Renaissance artists were aware of it as an esoteric tradition.[37] The two children became combined during the event described by Luke when the twelve-year-old Jesus and his family go to the Temple at Jerusalem, and afterwards Jesus is found to have been left behind. His parents return to find him discussing spiritual teachings with the rabbis in an extraordinarily wise manner. This was possible because the ego of the child born of the Solomon descent (as described in St Matthew's Gospel) entered the body of the child born of the Nathan line (St Luke's account). This ego being was that of the mighty teacher Zarathustra who had taught the ancient Persians and had had many incarnations acquiring a deep wisdom. His descending spirit was perceived by the Magi of Iran as a star, which led them to his place of rebirth. This ego of the former Zarathustra departed at the Baptism by John in the Jordan to allow the Christ Being to enter for the period of three years.

Following the Mystery of Golgotha, the Zarathustra ego continues to reincarnate and bears the name of the Master Jesus (as distinct from the Christ, the purely spiritual being). He becomes the guiding being for esoteric Christianity and was designated as the leading Master of the West alongside Christian Rosenkreutz. He is said by Steiner to have taught the Gnostics (we do not know under what name).[38] As Templar wisdom has sometimes been called 'Gnostic' and the Gnostic emblem of Abraxas was used as a seal by some of the leading figures, this may place the Master Jesus in a special relationship to them. Abraxas was an emblem used widely on seals and amulets; it comprises a figure with a rooster's head, human torso and snakes as legs, sometimes with seven stars. It was used to personify the Deity, the source of 365 emanations (in the Greek number system the letters of the name add up to 365) said to derive from the Hebrew *abra'kesa—hide the four*—alluding to the four-letter Tetragrammaton, the divine name. Tertullian (*c.* 160–*c.* 220), an early polemicist against heresy, wrote:

> Afterwards broke out the heretic Basilides [117–38, early Gnostic teacher in Alexandria]. He affirms that there is a supreme Deity, by name Abraxas, by whom was created Mind, which in Greek he calls Nous; that thence sprang the Word; that of Him issued Providence, Virtue and Wisdom; that out of these subsequently were made Principalities, Powers and Angels; that there ensued infinite issues and processions of angels; that by these angels 365 heavens were formed, and the world, in honour of Abraxas, whose name, if computed, has in itself this number. Now, among the last of the angels, those who made this world, he places the God of the Jews latest, that is, the God of the Law and of the Prophets, whom he denies to be a God, but affirms to be an angel.[39]

Thus we find a doctrine of creation that emanates through a hierarchy of cosmic beings, a belief common to Gnostics, Manichaeans and Kabbalists, though expressed in different terminologies. The imagery of the rooster is said to symbolize wisdom and vigilance as it crows to drive away the darkness as the sun rises. It was also a symbol of repentance (and of Peter's denial?). The initiate is reborn after the initiatory death of the night. The snakes symbolize the earthly forces to be overcome and transformed. The human torso bears a shield for the struggle to obtain wisdom. It sometimes bears the Greek letters I A Ω (later transcribed as 'W') (iota, alpha, omega) for protection. When used by some of the Masters of the Templars as a seal the emblem has the

A Templar Master's Abraxas seal from the thirteenth century

inscription *SECRETVM TEMPLI*, but as a seal it was used for stamping documents and not necessarily by a hidden elite. The emblem was used too widely in the Middle Ages to attract the attention of the Templars' inquisitors and thereby incur a further charge of heresy.

Rudolf Steiner describes an incarnation of the Master Jesus known to esoteric studies as that of the 'Friend of God from the Oberland (Highland), who appeared to Johannes Tauler and his companions in the late fourteenth century.[40] This is past the time of the Templars on earth, but the Master Jesus is described as being 'in continual incarnation'.[41] He leads souls in esoteric Christianity and guides them towards the next epoch, the sixth, the Aquarian age, to John the Baptist, the 'Waterman', and represents brotherly love.[42]

There is moreover a beautiful legend apparently in the Rosicrucian tradition that at every Eastertide this Master Jesus visits the place of the Mystery of Golgotha—whether or not he is actually incarnated. In fact, in a lecture of 5 May 1912 in Düsseldorf, Steiner speaks as if this is more than a legend—an event: 'For while sects of different kinds scattered over the earth are at strife among themselves, he through whom the greatest of all tidings of peace was brought to the earth looks again at the places that were the scene of his earthly deeds.'[43]

Since Jerusalem was held by the Templars until 1187 and they regained the use of the churches for brief periods until their final expulsion from the Holy Land, it is not difficult to imagine that those brothers whose esoteric development was greater were sometimes aware of this spiritual encounter at Easter. Such encounters were described by the Austrian poet Anastasias Grün in his long poem Five Easters, one of which was following the initial capture of Jerusalem by crusaders:

Where rises yon grey dome on rock foundation,
Through all the halls, in all the fields around,
Bristling in helm and mail, the congregation
Of brazen men throng to the trumpet's sound.

. . .

Ha! Will they go against their God in battle,
Whose holy house they thus in brass surround?
Ha! Will they storm the skies with war's wild rattle
Who at the temple's gates arms in are found?

But no! How suddenly the organ's pealing
Brings down that host in homage to the ground,
All heads are bowed, the haughty limbs are kneeling,
The iron fists against the breastplates sound,

I see on high, the cross of Christ, the holy,
Float from the temple's pinnacles, light and free;
All on their bosoms wear that ensign lowly,
Oh, that they, too, might each, God's temple be!

In all the colours of the rainbow beaming,
Stitched to their shirts of mail, the cross they wear,
Like living, walking, red cross standards gleaming
And lowered for solemn consecration there.

A thousand candles at the altar blazing,
The priest now breaks the consecrated bread,
Two blood-stained hands I plainly see him raising,
Not with the blood of Christ those hands are red!

At Sanctus, when he beat his breast confessing,
Beneath his chasuble a breastplate rung;
And, for the holy sprinkler, at the blessing,
Almost the sword, which stood nearby, he swung.

Next to the altar, reverently bending,
Kneels, on a velvet stool, a man alone;
Even on his knees, in beauty all transcending,
In sooth, erect, still fairer had he shone![44]

. . .

4. The Holy Grail

A connection between the Templars and the Holy Grail mystery has long been claimed. It usually takes the form of the Templars 'guarding' the Grail in some way and in more recent times this has been extended to include protecting certain bloodlines—a much more dubious interpretation. *San Graal* or *Sang Real* (Holy Grail or Holy Blood)? Blood and the Grail are intertwined as the legends have it that the chalice used at the Last Supper became also the vessel which caught the blood of Christ when his side was pierced by the Roman soldier's lance at the Crucifixion. Joseph of Arimathaea was the first 'guardian' of the cup and its contents, and there are many legends, alternative gospels and visionary experiences of his travels to France and Britain with the sacred treasure. There is a legend that the cup was formed from a stone fallen from Lucifer's crown when he was banished from the heavenly world, and in some versions this stone itself remains a stone, a sacred object capable of bringing about spiritual nourishment and transformation.

Human blood carries the force of the human 'I', and Christ's blood in the chalice contained the replica of the 'I' of Christ Jesus.[45] Rudolf Steiner has described the forming of the blood from the activity of the human ether or life body,[46] and says that Christ's blood was in its etheric component of a special 'unfallen' nature comprising the ethers withheld from humanity's usage— the forbidden fruit of the 'Tree of Life'.[47] Thus the container and the contained have both a special spiritual quality, a healing, nourishing, regenerating power, an 'unfallen' aspect that did not suffer the effect of Lucifer's activities and which remained in the care of spiritual beings until the time was right. This blood of Christ as it worked to transform the earth passed through a process of etherization—a returning to its etheric, non-physical state, but remaining within the etheric body of the earth. Our human blood also undergoes transformation back into etheric substance as it streams from the heart to the head.[48] If a person comes truly to understand the Christ and lets this understanding into the heart, this stream can meet and unite with Christ's etherized bloodstream. When Steiner describes the Templars' blood as 'belonging to Christ' we can imagine that this means that the knights' blood was brought into a 'resonance' with that of Christ's, and into which also streamed their strong will forces.

> The blood of the Templars belonged to Christ Jesus—each one of them knew this. . . . Every moment of their life was to be filled with the perpetual consciousness of how in their own soul there dwelt—in the words of St Paul—'not I, but Christ in me'! . . . Words are unable to describe what lived in the souls of these men, who were never allowed to flee, even if a force three times their strength confronted them on the physical plane, but who had calmly to await death . . . It was an intense life of the whole human being in union with the Mystery of Golgotha.[49]

In the light of this we can better understand Rudolf Steiner's words in an early lecture:

> The key thing to emerge from [the Crusades] were the Knights Templar, the actual messengers of the Grail. They built a centre of wisdom on the site of Solomon's Temple and after preparation there they became servants of the Holy Grail, were initiated there by the Grail.[50]

We are led deeper into the mystery of the blood. How might we understand being 'initiated by the Grail'? One key to understanding this comes from beyond the threshold of this world. During the First World War a young German woman began to receive 'messages' from her brother Sigwart who had been killed. These were shown to Steiner who considered them to be genuine communications from beyond the grave. One such message was as follows:

> I was present at the explanation of Parsifal . . . The basic thought pertains to Christ's blood, which has *actually transformed* the astral substance of the earth. Right after this occurrence events took place in the various layers surrounding

the earth. *This* was the transformation of the physical substances. Christ died for us, but *we* also died for Him. In the moment that the drops of His blood touched the earth the consciousness of humans descended into their 'etheric bodies' and beheld for a short duration of time the greatest event the earth was ever permitted to experience. Upon returning to their physical bodies they all had become knowing to a high degree. They felt it at first as a strong inner experience; it changed later to an unconscious sentiment of awe and magnificence. This feeling gradually weakened with the passing of the centuries, but the power of the inner voice remained as a nucleus that rests in *everyone*, becoming especially vocal in times of distress.[51]

It becomes possible for human beings to descend into their own etheric body and experience the effect of Christ's blood. We can imagine that the founding knights especially would have attempted this during their time in Jerusalem.

It was also a task of certain of the dead to become guardians of the Grail. Such souls would work together with those still on earth—for example the Order of the Swan was set up for this purpose.[52] Lohengrin, the son of Parzival, is called the Swan Knight. Manfred Schmidt-Brabant has suggested that the image of two knights riding one horse, as seen on several Templar seals, was not an image of poverty (for in fact every knight was allowed three horses) but of the working together of a soul beyond the grave with the brother on earth.[53]

The stories of the search for the Holy Grail form the core of the Arthurian legends of the Middle Ages and have come down to us in various forms. Steiner revealed to W.J. Stein especially that historical personalities were in fact concealed behind some of the familiar names, and that specific initiations had occurred during the ninth century.[54] The original knights of King Arthur were concerned with understanding the secrets of the cosmos and of nature, and also were working to tame unruly human passions. The Grail knights, however, were the ones carrying the understanding of Christ's deed in their hearts and blood. During the ninth century the two streams united, though the stories concerning the quests did not appear in writing until the twelfth and thirteenth centuries. The quest of Parzival (Perceval) is probably the best known and in Wolfram von Eschenbach's epic the knights who guard the Grail castle are called Templars— *Templeisen*. This has led some authorities to question the translation as 'Templars' but other research shows that the Aragonese-Catalan word for Templars was *templés,* and this was rendered by Wolfram as *Templeis, Templeisen.*[55] If the events of the Parzival story do belong to the ninth century, then it may be questioned whether the Grail keepers could really be Templars as outer history tells us that the Order was not founded until 1118 or 1119. Herein lies the mystery of other possible ante-cedents or orders that may have been behind the setting up of the Order. (We can forget the spurious Priory of Sion, certainly in its present manifestation, now shown to have been founded in 1956![56]) In lectures on Richard Wagner's *Parsifal* Steiner refers to 'an important mystery centre [which] existed in a region of northern Spain at the time when the Crusades began and *a little before that* [author's emphasis]. The mysteries of those times were called "late Gothic mysteries". Their initiates were called Tempelisen or Tempeleisen or Knights of the Holy Grail. Lohengrin was one of them.'[57]

'The Swan Knight therefore appears to us as an emissary of the great White Brotherhood. Thus Lohengrin is the messenger of the Holy Grail.'[58] It may thus be possible to conclude that an earlier, more secret order of some kind did exist, which led to the creation of the Order of the Knights Templar somewhat later. We can imagine that the mystery of Christ's blood would have been a significant focus for its esoteric teaching. It appears that these mysteries may have been found in northern Spain espe-cially, for in addition to the reference above there are other allusions to the Grail castle hovering spiritually, so to speak, above this region.[59] Steiner's emphasis is less on a building of stone or wood but rather on a spiritual 'temple', in the same way that the Grail is not to be thought of as a physical vessel. And though Jerusalem was undoubtedly the centre of the mystery of

Christ's blood, it did not live on as a Christian centre. Spiritual powers could be active in other regions also and northern Spain, though significant, is not the only Grail mystery site. It has been suggested that these sites arose because Joseph of Arimathaea visited these locations and released a drop of Christ's blood into the ground there.[60] Whether such a physical act took place is less important—the imagination of a sacred space, a Grail castle, has been imprinted into souls in Europe (and now beyond) from the early Middle Ages onwards, and we can connect with such a 'castle' whenever we read or meditate on the stories and their characters.

In Wolfram's account, dating from the early thirteenth century, a strong emphasis is placed on brotherhood. Parzival is denied the Grail kingship until he learns to ask whom it serves and what ails the sick king. He must develop compassion and empathy. Then he learns of the existence of his half-brother Feirefis, a Muslim, whom he fights at first, but then embraces and is determined to lead to the Grail castle. Feirefis begins to love the Grail bearer, Repanse de Schoie, and thus comes to the mystery of Christ through this love. He can see her but not the Grail itself until he recognizes Christ. For the Templars, whose desire was to recognize their brother in the Saracen, this version must have proved especially meaningful. Although the Saracens were deemed the enemy, the knights were often accused of being too fraternal towards them, and indeed some people even blamed the loss of the Holy Land on supposed traitors—consorting with the 'infidel' and even incorporating certain possible Sufi beliefs. It is hard to imagine how they could have borne their destiny without a cult of spiritual love, a more mystical heart-centred practice and therefore may have added or at least appreciated Sufi ideas together with their Christian practices.

The version by Chrétien de Troyes stresses knighthood as a chivalrous ideal. He dedicated the work to Philip, Count of Flanders, claiming that Philip had given him the source of it. Philip was the son of Dietrich of Alsace and had inherited a relic, an alleged sample of Christ's blood given to Dietrich by Baldwin III of Jerusalem. Dietrich took part in the Second Crusade, inspired by St Bernard of Clairvaux. Hughes de Troyes, Count of Champagne was the overlord of Hugh de Payen, one of the founding knights. He provided the land for St Bernard's Abbey of Clairvaux. André de Montbard, another of the original nine, was also his vassal. Thus there were historical links between the transmission of the Grail story and the Templar Order.

It is, however, perhaps the version known as *The Quest of the Holy Grail (Queste del Saint Graal)*[61] that carries a particular relevance. Its author claims to be Walter Map, Archdeacon of Oxford and protégé of Henry II, but as he died in 1209 and scholars have dated this cycle somewhere between 1215 and 1230, this may be untrue. But there is some consensus that this version had a connection with the Cistercian Order especially, and is thought to be part of the Vulgate Cycle commissioned by St Bernard. Anna Morduch writes in *The Sovereign Adventure*:

St Bernard, the great protector of the Knights Templar ... gave to his spiritual sons much more than the rules of the newly-founded militia. He gave them in his book *In Praise of the New Militia* stations of contemplation and inner training, which can be found in vivid pictures and parables in the *Queste del Saint Graal*.[62]

It is within this text that we can find particular references, which would have been meaningful to those within or familiar with the Order. On p. 97 of the 1975 Penguin edition there is a reference to the 'Templar' psalm, no. 133, quoted by the aunt of Perceval (a character who takes the place of Sigune in Wolfram's version, and admonishes him for leaving his mother broken-hearted):

You are well aware that since the advent of Jesus Christ the world has seen three great fellowships. The first was the table of Jesus Christ, where the apostles broke bread on many occasions. That was the table where the bread of heaven sustained both souls and bodies, while they that sat around it were one in heart and soul, as King David prophesied when he wrote in his book the wonderful words: 'Behold, how good and how pleasant it is for brethren to dwell together in unity.'

[Psalm 133]... Thereafter there was instituted another table in memory of the Holy Grail which, in the days of Joseph of Arimathea when the Christian faith was first brought to this land, saw the enacting of miracles so great that godly men and unbelievers both should ever hold them in remembrance... This table was succeeded by the Round Table, devised by Merlin to embody a very subtle meaning. For in its name it mirrors the roundness of the earth, the concentric spheres of the planets and of the elements in the firmament; and in these heavenly spheres we see the stars and many things besides; whence it follows that the Round Table is a true epitome of the universe. From every land, be it Christian or heathen, where chivalry resides, knights are seen flocking to the Round Table. And when by God's grace they are made companions, they count themselves richer than if they had gained the whole world, and to this end forsake father, mother, wife and children too... When Merlin had established the Round Table, he announced that the secret of the Holy Grail, which in his time was covert and withdrawn, would be revealed by knights of that same fellowship.

Thus the Last Supper, the story of Joseph of Arimathaea and the Round Table all become united in an image of brotherhood and Christian mystery: 'There were many in the circle of the Knights Templar who could gain a deep insight into the Mystery of Golgotha and its meaning and into Christian symbolism as it had taken shape through the development of the Last Supper.'[63] At the Grail castle *nine* knights converge to join Galahad, Perceval and Bors, the three deemed holy enough to perceive the Grail. The twelve partake of a ceremony resembling the Mass, during which Christ manifests in the Holy Vessel. Galahad, the virgin son of Lancelot, is the main protagonist of this version—perhaps because he was traditionally celibate. He acquires the shield 'with a red cross on a white ground', which was stated to have been made for none other than him. Other noteworthy images are the healing power of Perceval's sister's blood, and that the maimed king, when healed finally by the blood from the holy lance with which Galahad anoints his legs, enters a 'monastery of white monks'. The whole tone of this version is more lofty and monastic and perhaps less appealing today than Wolfram's lively tale, but with references to St John's Gospel and also to the Song of Solomon it carries an important esoteric undertone that would very likely have found favour with the Order. Its mystery of the 'holy blood' is strongly emphasized, female characters bear this too—perhaps in honour of the Virgin Mary—and images abound of spiritual states of being, conveying the required mood of those times for penetrating 'through the veil' (Perceval also means 'pierce the vale'). In an image of a ship crossing the sea—entering an 'astral body' state—Galahad, Perceval and Bors journey with the Grail to Sarras, the New Jerusalem, where the Grail displays its miraculous healing powers. Galahad and Perceval die there but Bors returns to this world, to Camelot and King Arthur to relate the tale.

To reach a deeper understanding of these connections we must lay aside the desire for historical proof, documentary evidence, which is unlikely to be forthcoming; but by entering into the imaginations of the stories we can come to feel that heart connection, which surely was an inspiration to the knights.

5. Mani

Rudolf Steiner placed the Templar Order firmly in the Manichaean stream, although this is not mentioned in historical records.[64] Mani (or Manes) was the third-century founder of a branch of Christianity unusual enough to be regarded as non-Christian by some historians, probably because of the Zoroastrian influence. Stories of Mani's life vary.[65] But it is generally accepted that he was born on 14 April 216 in Babylon (Iraq) and is thought to have been raised in a Gnostic Jewish-Christian sect, the Elchasaites. Aged 12, he received a revelation from a being he called 'the Twin'—his higher angelic self, who reappeared when he was 24, sending him out into the world with his newly found understanding. He took the name Mani (having been known as Kurkabios), meaning Manas-bearer, or bearer of the Spirit Self, the next higher stage of human consciousness towards which we are evolving. He gathered followers and his teaching spread across Asia to the far East, including China and probably Japan. Initially supported in this by King Shapur I of Iran, he later fell foul of the latter's descendent Barham and the Zoroastrian priesthood. He was imprisoned as a traitor, tortured and died in prison aged 60 in AD 277. His teaching is mainly concerned with the *problem of evil*. He described evil as having come into the world at the same time as good—he does not appear to have traced an origin back further. Elaborate myths describe the assault on good by evil, but unlike the Gnostic teachings in which evil was to be kept firmly at bay, and the true follower would achieve gnosis in an exclusive state of purity, Mani taught that there was 'light' within every being, which could eventually be rescued and redeemed. When we come to consider the nature of 'Baphomet', this may become clearer. Steiner spoke of a future period when evil can be transformed by the power of thought;[66] we have not yet reached this stage but preparations have been and are being made. We learn that Mani reincarnated as the historical figure behind Parzival.[67] In Wolfram von Eschenbach's version of the story, Parzival does not claim the right to be Grail king until he has brought his half-brother Feirefis, a Muslim, to the Grail castle. Feirefis cannot see the Grail but beholds the Grail bearer, Repanse de Schoie and, filled with love for her, chooses to follow Christ and discover the Grail. (The deeper connection to the Grail legends is explored in the previous chapter.)

In what way were the Templars Manichaean? In the near East and Spain especially, they were said to have sought meetings with followers of other faiths—Jewish and Muslim—for mutual instruction and understanding. Their external aim was to protect the holy sites, not to kill the Saracen (unfortunately the less enlightened crusaders took a different view) and though this was not the original intention battles inevitably arose and massacres took place. At the trials, and even beforehand, they were accused of being too friendly towards the Saracen 'enemy' and blamed for losing control of the Holy Land. In Part Two we will look at the question of the so-called 'secret statutes' of the Order, in which meetings with other faiths were consciously to be sought out. Although in its present form this is almost certainly a forgery, there is good reason to allow the idea that some form of mutual understanding was pursued.

Another aspect is the Templars' understanding of the nature of sacred sites—their geometry and geomancy. By building churches on 'power places' and by the daily spiritual practices therein, they were helping to transform the earth's energy flow. Of course other churches and religious orders took part in this work too, but the Templars seem to have wrought a transformation that even today can be felt in certain of their churches. For instance, in Shipley and Sompting churches in Sussex this has been felt and remarked upon by observers unaware of this aspect of their history. This may be because, as stated earlier, the brothers dedicated their blood to Christ:

In their blood, as the agent of that which distinguishes the earthly human being, in their 'I'—but also in all their feeling and thinking, in their very being and existence—these souls were, in a sense, to forget their connection with sensory physical existence. They had to live solely in what streams from the Mystery of Golgotha...[68]

They were able to work into their bloodstream so that it achieved a more 'etherized' state, a return to a more pristine state of life force, in which it could unite with the etherized blood of Christ. Guenther Wachsmuth has shown how the globe of the earth can be compared to a human blood corpuscle:

> ...we can study the configuration of the etheric body of the earth which is a reflection of our own inner being and we must realize that the etheric forces moulding the body of the earth are the same as those in our blood corpuscles ... when a change takes place in the etheric structure of human blood, this will be reflected into the etheric sphere of the earth, because, in effect, the earth and the blood corpuscles are formed according to the same laws.[69]

Thus by transforming their blood, the knights could work on effecting a transformation of the earth itself.

Because of their connection to the Manichaean stream and its future redemption of evil, Steiner has described how the Templars became a focus for one of the most evil adversaries, the Antichrist or Sun Demon, Sorat, the two-horned beast of the Apocalypse. With his special manifestations *c.* AD 666 and its multiples—*c.* 1338 (the exact date need not be precise) he sought to destroy the spirituality of the Order from within by entering into souls loosened from their bodies under torture during the Order's downfall.[70] Thus the more unusual or controversial practices (see Part Two) became distorted into something more sacrilegious and blasphemous than was necessarily the case. Nowadays enlightened people recognize the fallacy of information gained through torture, but such psychological awareness was uncommon during the Middle Ages.

After the death of Mani, Manichaean beliefs and practices continued in the far East for many centuries, but in addition a number of so-called heretical sects developed in Europe and the Byzantine Empire through to the late Middle Ages, which are often labelled 'Manichaean'.[71] They were considered heretical because they practised a Christianity which recognized a cosmology in which a hierarchy of spiritual beings from cosmic realms had brought about a series of processes in evolution and were the beings who belonged to the Godhead, although in some sects the earth itself was seen as a product of an adversary. Moreover, the Christ was a cosmic Being who descended into the body of Jesus. These Gnostic (in the widest sense) beliefs had been suppressed by the Roman Church in the early Christian centuries but had survived in small pockets, especially in the near East. Certain ideas were common among both Gnostic and Manichaean offshoots, such as the Docetists, who refused to accept that the Christ could really have entered a human body, gone through death and resurrected (the most essential tenet of Christianity), and there were those who believed that Jesus may or may not have been merely human, not divine, or may not have really died on the cross, which resulted in a loathing for the symbol of the crucifix. We shall be looking at how this may have penetrated the Templar rituals in some form.

By the Middle Ages these movements were once more gaining ground. The Cathars, the best known, may be more Gnostic than Manichaean—at least in their further development—as the aim became to leave the earth behind because they thought it had been created by an evil being, so much so that a form of suicide through self-starvation, the *endura,* was practised by the more advanced adherents. Other sects were the Bogomils, Paulicians, Messalians, Patarenes. The Paulicians, probably so named for a special reverence for St Paul, arose chiefly in Armenia and certainly came into contact with the crusaders in the Near East. Beliefs that the earth was in some measure a creation of evil beings (they were labelled 'dualist') seem to have been held in common, and there was uncertainty about the being of Jesus and his relation to the indwelling Christ resulting in an abhorrence of the cross. The 'teaching of light' was strong in Syria as well as in northern Arabia, Egypt and North Africa. From Syria it spread to Palestine, Asia Minor and Armenia. In spite of the later Muslim advances into most of these regions, some aspects of these more esoteric Christian beliefs lingered there to be encountered by the knights serving there, and also in southern France and northern Italy where Catharism was widely practised and many Templars had Cathar family connections and supported their cause. The following sects are mentioned, for instance, in the 'secret statutes' as ones which the initiated brothers should seek out:[72] the *Good Men of Toulouse* (Bon-hommes), a name given to the Cathar Perfects but sometimes used for the whole sect; the *Poor of Lyon* (the Waldensians of Lyon who were considered heretical though they were not dualists, i.e. conceiving of good and evil as equal powers in the universe); the *Albigenses*, usually Cathar but sometimes applied to all 'heretics'; *those in the neighbourhood of Verona* (there were six Cathar churches there in 1250) *and Bergamo* (probably followers of the thirteenth-century heretic bishop John Lugio of Bergamo who preached 'unqualified dualism'); the *Bajolais of Galicia and Tuscany* (probably the Baiolensis or Bagnolenses, Cathars from Lombardy and Tuscany); the *Bégards* who, like the *Béguines*, were religious communities found more in northern Europe and also accused of heresy and free spiritual beliefs (interestingly, they were condemned at the Council of Vienne (1311–12) together with the Templars, and though they did not share the Templars' terrible fate they were required to join minor Franciscan orders); the *Bulgars* or Bogomils from Bulgaria. The Bulgars had connections with the French Cathars. 'Bulgar' or 'Bougre' was freely used for the heresy in thirteenth century France, and later corrupted to the expletive. Whether all these were strictly part of the Manichaean stream is open to question, but Docetist or dualist beliefs and a desire for a Christianity free from the oppressive Roman Church hierarchy were uniting features.

Mani's doctrine featured the struggle between light and darkness (the Zoroastrian influence), but he differed from the Iranian beliefs by teaching how light came to mingle with darkness and, by gradually redeeming it, a new kind of light would emerge, known as the 'column of glory', demonstrated by 'Jesus the Saviour' or 'Jesus the Splendour'. The actual myth was quite complicated but the aim is to release as much light as possible by love and care for all beings of creation and to work on rescuing one's own light from inner darkness. In China Manichaeism was actually known as the 'Religion of Light', involving the term *Ming*, embodying light and life in the sense of St John's Prologue.

In the chapter on St John the Evangelist we mentioned the mystery of the 'John' figures. An interesting Manichaean text on the suffering of the righteous, including Jesus and the apostles, states:

> The two sons of Zebedee were made to drink the cup of the . . .
>   [gap in text]
> John the virgin, he also was made to drink the cup,
> Fourteen days imprisoned that he might die of (hunger);
> And James also, he was stoned and killed . . . [73]

Thus a John is mentioned apparently in addition to John Zebedee—possible evidence for this mystery knowledge being extant among the more esoteric Christian sects.

Manichaean communities were permitted to acquire wealth and capital in the form of debentures. Lending on credit or usury was thus not forbidden, a fact which may have paved the way for the Templars' banking and credit services.

Manichaeans were strict about diet and considered certain plants and vegetables to be more 'light filled' than others. These were especially cucumbers and melons. It is interesting to note that people suffering from a gall or liver dysfunction often cannot tolerate these—as if their own gall is maybe too bitter or 'dark'. The rescued light from food (animal matter was not consumed) was delivered from the admixture of darkness or matter and enriched, especially in the *elect*—those Manichaeans who, like the Cathar Perfect, entered into the full teachings.

6. St Mark

St Mark the Evangelist is not normally associated with the Templars. He was not one of the twelve, but was a pupil of Peter. His Gospel is thought to have been the earliest written down in approximately AD 65–70, and he added material from conversations with Peter in Rome. It does not appear to be like the more esoteric Gospel of St John, but in recent times material has come to light showing that he may also have been transmitting a more secret line of mystery wisdom. In Freemasonry, the Rite of Misraim (later combined with that of Memphis) traces its origin back to the Egyptian Mysteries. In his lessons for his cultic-ritual esoteric school at the beginning of the twentieth century, Rudolf Steiner stated that when Mark became Bishop of Alexandria he worked with an Egyptian initiate of the Mysteries of Isis called Ormus, who became a Christian, and together they were 'pupils [disciples] of the Christ since his resurrection'. Steiner claimed that the Misraim Service (*Misraim Dienst*), which he introduced, had descended from Mark's teachings.[74] The story of Mark and Ormus is often treated dismissively by some writers on Freemasonry, apart from Lynn Picknett and Clive Prince in *The Sion Revelation*, who refer to Ormus having founded the 'Brothers of Ormus', which became joined by a Jewish stream of 'Solomonic science'.[75] The Brothers of Ormus were also known as the Rosicrucians of the East. The Order of the Golden and Rosy Cross founded in the late 1790s by the German Freemason Hermann Fichtuld also claims an origin from Ormus. It claims too that members initiated the Templars in Palestine in 1188, that Masters thereafter founded the Order of the Masons of the East in Scotland (pre-dating the supposed transmission following the fall of the Templars), and that Ramon Lull (Raymond Lully), the Spanish esoteric philosopher, was a member.[76] The Ormus tradition, too, has been used as a basis for the somewhat notorious 'Priory of Sion', now established as having been founded with political aims in 1956.[77]

The esoteric side of Mark's teaching might have remained the

stuff of legend had there not been a remarkable discovery made
by Morton Smith, an American scholar, in 1958 in the Judean
monastery of Mar Saba.[78] He discovered a letter from the
Church Father Clement of Alexandria quoting from what was
said to be the original version of the Gospel of Mark—the one
we have today being the expurgated version. The original one is
said to have contained 'secret teachings' which, according to
Clement, were being misused by Christian sects such as the
Carpocratians (who believed that satisfying sins was a means of
salvation) and consequently certain passages were removed from
the canonical gospel. The passage quoted is a striking one
referring to Christ's raising of Lazarus, a miracle which only
appears in St John's Gospel. The 'secret gospel' makes it clear
that this was a mystery event, an initiation, rather than a raising
from the dead, which is what Steiner declared in his *Christianity
as Mystical Fact.*

> And going out of the tomb, they came to the house which
> belonged to the youth—for he was rich. And after six days,
> Jesus told him what to do, and in the evening the youth came
> to him, wearing nothing but a linen cloth. And he remained
> with him that night. For Jesus taught him the mystery of the
> kingdom of God.[79]

Lazarus, like Nicodemus, comes 'by night', a Mystery designation. It must be said, though, that the authenticity of this letter
of Clement's is not certain and some scholars dispute it.

The Coptic Church of North Africa is said to have descended
from St Mark's teachings. During the lifetime of Mani, his pupil
Herman spread Manichaeism to Egypt, and it often became
mingled with the Coptic beliefs. The designation of the 'son of
the widow' has its origin here, from the Isis Mysteries, and is
common to both Manichaeans and Freemasons. Isabel Cooper-
Oakley quotes Karl Roessler (*History of Freemasonry*, Leipzig
1836) stating that these Coptic mysteries were transmitted to the
nine founders of the Templar Order by the Bishop of Upsala.[80]
Certainly equal-armed *croix patées*—the Templar cross—can be
seen in Coptic religious art.

Another strange document purporting to show Templar descent from the Copts is the *Lévitikon*, a document which Bernard Raymond Fabré-Palaprat, who founded the Order of the Temple in 1804, claimed to have discovered on a second-hand bookstall in Paris. Masonic historian Aimée Bothwell-Gosse (1866–1954), however, claims it had belonged to the Paris Temple and has been authenticated as medieval.[81] This document states how Jesus received all the initiation degrees in Egypt and initiated disciples, especially John, who passed these mysteries to his successors. A list of these includes the Patriarch Théoclet, who in 1099 conferred them on Hughes de Payen, one of the founding brothers in 1118 (Théoclet does not appear to be known outside this tradition). Garimond was the Latin Patriarch of Jerusalem who invested Hughes de Payen and Geoffrey de Saint-Omer in 1118 (or 1119). The mysteries, it is claimed, were passed to the successive Grand Masters until the last one, Jacques de Molay, who was said to have invested Jean-Marc Larmenius in 1307 (or 1314) before his death. A further succession of Grand Masters was added by Fabré-Palaprat. It is sometimes called the Larmenius Transmission in the 'Johannite tradition' (the other transmission or Templar survival being the Scottish Rite). The document includes the Gospel of St John but with only 19 chapters; the resurrection is omitted. As this gives the whole meaning to Christianity both exoteric and esoteric, it renders the Lévitikon rather spurious, a possible forgery bent on perpetuating the idea that Christ did not really pass through death, being of a spiritual nature entirely which did not unite with the human body of Jesus and thus having no need to resurrect. It claims, moreover, that the teachings had nine grades, called *Levites*:

1) Guard or warder of exterior defence, knight
2) Levite of the Temple
3) Levite of the interior door
4) Levite of the Sanctuary
5) Ceremonial Levite
6) Levite theological

7) Levite deacon
8) Levite priest, doctor of law
9) Levite pontiff or bishop

These apparently passed to the Templars but none of it is in any surviving Templar documentation.

The purpose of this inclusion is not to give it credence but to show that the idea of a Coptic-Markian origin for esoteric Christian beliefs may have had a connection to the founding of the Order and there is some reason for considering St Mark as an inspirer.

Part Two
RITUALS AND BELIEFS

7. Templar Rituals

Here we are in territory very difficult to fathom, as no other order has probably inspired so much speculation, disinformation and outright fantasy. The problem is that most historical knowledge comes from the records of the Templar trials—information received from men under torture or in a desperate state. Any written records by the Templars themselves are thought to have perished in Cyprus, when the archive, such as it was by then, was destroyed by the Turks in 1571. We must now tread through some of the murkier pages of history.

Depositions from the trials included references to a secret inner Order with closed chapters, and to a mysterious second reception in which the brother was required to spit, trample or defile the cross, receive kisses on private parts of his body, accept possible homosexual acts, and show reverence for an idol or statue, a head or figure, sometimes known as Baphomet. (This latter warrants a chapter to itself.) In some cases the brother also had to deny that Jesus was divine or had died on the cross. Accusations that the knights wore a magic cord or worshipped a cat are not worth serious consideration.

A concealed group within the Order seems well attested. For instance Rudolf Steiner told Eleanor Merry that the British leading anthroposophist Daniel Dunlop had belonged to a secret Order within the Templars.[82] That such a group held closed chapters, probably at night, is hardly surprising. Such a group may not have been open to all knights—though a number who were interrogated give confused accounts of having been inducted especially with the 'denial of the cross'. We have something of a puzzle here. On the one hand Steiner spoke of how the Templars under torture were taken over by the demonic entity Sorat,[83] who caused them to admit to deeds that they had not performed or fallen to temptations they had overcome:

When you can see into what went on in the souls of the Templars while they were being tortured you can gain some idea of how what lived in their visions was instigated by Sorat. As a result they slandered themselves, providing their enemies with a cheap indictment through what they themselves uttered. People were confronted with the terrible spectacle of seeing individuals being unable to speak about what they genuinely represented, while different spirits from among the cohorts of Sorat spoke through them instead, accusing the Order of the most disgusting things out of the mouths of its own adherents.[84]

Many a one who in consequence of his Christian initiation could look into the Christian impulses passing through the historical evolution of the European peoples also saw something else; he experienced it in his own soul, as it were, since it always again came over him as a temptation. Recognizing the unconscious capabilities of the human soul, he repeatedly overcame the temptation that showed itself to him. The initiated thus became conscious of it and sought to overcome what otherwise remained in the subconscious. Many knights learned to know the devilish urge that takes possession of the will and feeling to debase the Mystery of Golgotha. In the dream pictures by which many such initiates were haunted, there appeared in vision the reverse of the veneration of the symbol of the crucifix. This was possible owing to the way in which the initiation had come about, and particularly because the Luciferic forces had stood close by with their temptation.[85]

Therefore both ahrimanic-Sorat and luciferic forces combined to attack the Order. In an earlier lecture, however, Steiner puts forward a rather different perspective:

Moreover, the Templars said: Today we live at a point in time when human beings are not yet ripe for understanding the great teachings; we still have to prepare them for the Baptist, John, who baptizes with water. The cross was held up before the would-be Templar and he was told: You must deny the cross now so as to understand it later; first become a Peter, first deny the scriptures, like Peter the Rock who denied the

Lord. That was imparted to the aspirant Templar as a pre-
liminary training.[86]

Here the knights went through the experience of denying the
cross, becoming a 'Peter' denying Christ, in order to affirm him
more strongly later. This in fact is what Geoffrey de Gonneville,
preceptor of Aquitaine and Poitou, stated in his trial.[87] One
explanation for this apparent contradiction is that Steiner was
addressing rather different groups of people. In the second
example (1905), he was speaking to members of the Theosophical Society, who were probably also members of his Esoteric School, and who had a background in symbolic esotericism
and in some cases ritual work and could grasp this kind of rite.
In the first passage (1916), the listeners were a much more mixed
group of members of the Anthroposophical Society, probably
people from very different karmic backgrounds who did not
always have the same degree of esoteric understanding. Here
Rudolf Steiner seems to have been anxious to 'clear the name' of
the Templars and wanted to emphasize a different view of them
which stressed their devotion and allegiance to Christ—we can
only surmise that this was important because he could see the
karmic past of some of the listeners.

In the evidence of Stephen of Stapelbridge (Stephen de Sta-
pelbrugge) of England, we have someone who was probably not
tortured—at least it may have been more of a 'roughing up' than
the systematic and cruel torments the French knights had to
undergo, as Edward II would not at first allow torture. Historians have not found records that torture ever took place even
when finally the king gave in to pressure from Philip the Fair and
Pope Clement. But we should not of course underestimate the
extreme distress and soul confusion experienced by the knights,
used to being treated with respect, suddenly held in captivity and
accused of terrible antichristian deeds. Stephen of Stapelbridge
refers to two receptions, one 'good' and one 'bad'.[88] In the
second, he was asked to deny Jesus as God and to spit upon the
cross, so he spat on a hand next to it. Thus there may well have
been a further ritual in which the brother had to undergo a

'denial like Peter' experience, and not all of them may have understood it properly. Whether they did or not, under torture or in psychological distress anyway, they felt they had committed a foul deed, enhanced by the machinations of the adversary forces, and presented a distorted picture of what had taken place. Steiner's description in the lecture of 1905 of three stages of purification makes clear that hindering forces brought about a false interpretation of a ritual rather than giving rise to a complete fantasy.

> ... the human being still has to undergo three stages of purification. The ego is in a threefold sheath: firstly, in the astral body; secondly, in the etheric body; thirdly in the physical body. When we are in the astral body, we deny the divine ego for the first time, we do so for the second time in the etheric body, and for the third time in the physical body. The first crow of the cock is threefold denial through the threefold sheath of the human being. And when he has then passed through the three bodies, when the ego discovers in Christ its greatest symbolic realization, then the cock crows for the second time.
>
> None of the Templars who were put under torture at that time were able to convey these profound thoughts to their judges—this struggle to raise oneself up to a proper understanding of Christ, first passing through the stage of Peter.[89]

This may also be another explanation for the cockerel's head on the Gnostic emblem of Abraxas.

The accusation of licence to practise sodomy would seem to fall into the category of how the Templars who were tortured experienced the feeling that they may have actually done what they fought to overcome in themselves:

> During their torture, the vision of the Templars that could look out over these spiritual worlds to which they belonged became clouded and dim, their surface consciousness was dulled, and their inner gaze was directed entirely and only to what they had experienced as something to be overcome; was

directed to the temptations over which they had gained victory after victory... The Trials and temptations which they had resisted and overcome stood before them, as a vision, while they lay stretched on the rack. And they acknowledged the very thing that each one for himself had overcome, they confessed it to be a custom within the Order.[90]

The misunderstanding of the so-called obscene kisses may have occurred likewise. It has been suggested that the purpose of these was to acknowledge the chakra points of the human body as part of the purification rituals, to mark what must be transformed in the lower nature. Carlo Pietzner described a possible version of the ritual in a lecture he gave at Copake in 1966.[91] He had clearly read the 'secret statutes' and reinterprets them very beautifully. It is possible that an actual 'secret' document did once exist, but what we have now is highly embellished and spurious, as the next chapter shows. In fact, some of the trial depositions do refer to a secret rule existing in some written form. Etienne de Troyes, who in fact had left the Order, was a witness at Poitiers, and even if not actually tortured was probably threatened and frightened into making a confession, for he claims also that he was importuned for homosexual purposes and when he brought this to Hughes de Pairaud

> ... he was told that the brother had done well, since indeed he ought not to deny himself. Beyond this he had heard that the points concerning the denial of Christ and the other things were in the Rule of the Order, which the Visitor held. Brothers could only be received according to this Rule, which was guarded by the great men of the Order, and the younger men were prevented from seeing it.[92]

Raoul de Presles was evidently a secular witness, one of 20 selected and controlled by Philip the Fair:

> Raoul de Presles told the commissioners that when he had lived in Laon ... he had been very friendly with Gervais de Beauvais, preceptor of the local house. This brother had frequently said—indeed over a hundred times—that there was a

point in the Order so secret that he would rather have his head cut off than tell anyone. There was also a point in the general chapter of the Order which was so secret that if Raoul de Presles or even the King of France should see it, those holding the chapter would seek to kill them, deferring to the authority of no one in this. Furthermore, Gervais had said that the Order had a small book of statutes which he would show to Presles willingly, but there existed another secret book which he would not show for all the world.[93]

Unfortunately, due to the corrupt conditions under which the trials were held, these witnesses may not be given much credence. But it is interesting that there were *rumours* of a secret document at a period when written material was scanty, though such authentic original documents have not so far come to light.

8. The 'Secret Statutes'

What do we have by way of information about the Templar Order besides reports of the trials? We have the legendary accounts of the Order's history as already cited, some individuals' visionary experiences and the so-called secret statutes. The account of the origin of the 'secret statutes' claims that Frederik Münter, a Danish scholar and Bishop of Zeeland (1762–1830), went to Rome and was given permission to study the Vatican archives, where he claimed to have discovered them. He bequeathed his papers to Wilke, saying they were incomplete. He thought the Templars were good Catholics but also Paulician and Gnostics and Wilke should be careful not to accuse them of heresy. The document was copied and taken to Copenhagen, St Petersburg and Stockholm and returned to St Petersburg where it was kept until 1860 before being passed to Dr Buck of Hamburg. He left his papers to the Grand Lodge of Hamburg where Theodore Merzdorf found the document and translated it from the Latin in 1877. French translations can be found in books by René Gilles and Gérard de Serbanesco, in German by Theodore Merzdorf and in uncertain English on the Internet.[94]

This dubious Masonic history alone casts doubt on their authenticity and they will not consequently be printed here in full. Nonetheless their existence is now part of Templar history and, I believe, worth examining. We can always learn something from *shadows* that are cast.

They comprise two sets of articles, those of the *Elect Brothers,* and those of the *Consoled Brothers,* the latter rite referred to as the *Book of the Baptism of Fire.* A further document, not included in Serbanesco's account, describes certain ritual signs, Masonic-type signs. The whole tone is vehemently anti Roman Church, much is made of the necessity to meet with Muslims and Jews as well as so-called heretics and to avoid the Church of Rome. How this was to square with the allegiance to the Pope promised by the knights is not explained. The rites had to take place in secret nocturnal chapters. The reception of the Elect describes in Article 11: 'The one receiving shall kiss in turn the neophyte on the mouth, to transmit the breath to him, on the sacral plexus which controls the creative force, on the umbilical and finally on the virile member, the image of the male creative principle.' Thus arose the accusation of obscene kisses. Even if these were intended to mark out those forces that had to be overcome and transformed, this is naturally, even today, a highly controversial practice. Such rites play no part in normal religious rituals and are usually associated with magical or tantric sex practices. It should be remembered that certain Gnostic groups in the early Christian centuries were also accused of mingling sexual activity with spiritual observances. Article 13 describes the by now well-known accusation: 'The neophyte will trample the cross underfoot and will spit upon it.' This ritual features in several of the trial testimonies.

The Elect brothers are exhorted to study certain texts, some of which had something controversial about them from the Church's point of view, such as David of Dinant (c. 1160–c. 1217), a pantheistic philosopher condemned for his writings and forced to flee Paris. Anselm of Canterbury (1033–1109) and John of Salisbury (1120–80) were, however, more widely revered and accepted. The point, however, is that not all the knights were necessarily literate, for example Geoffrey de Gonneville, tried at Chinon in August 1308, claimed illiteracy, and he was a Preceptor.[95] Those responsible for keeping financial records, overseeing legal transactions, deeds of transfer, etc. must have had some literacy, but these were not learned monks who had time to study in their quiet cloisters, nor to regard theology as part of their remit. Article 29 permits the swearing of ignorance and denial of the secret rites and statutes. Article 30 stresses that a dying Elect brother should not be left alone but the company of another Elect should be sought to hear his confession. The hearing of confessions and granting of absolution by brothers other than a chaplain was another accusation made against the Order.

The first part closes by stating that the statutes were copied by Mathieu de Tramlay, St Felix Day 1205. Other names were added: Robert de Samfort, the 'Grand Master of the English Province' in 1235 and Master Roncelinus (Roncelin de Fos), Master in Provence until *c.* 1280. We will return to these names later.

The *Book of the Baptism of Fire* comprises 20 articles and exhorts the brothers to mix with Jews and Saracens and with the 'heretics' described in the chapter on Mani:

> Article 6. Among the Jews and Saracens, be as if you were Saracen or Jew. With the sons of Babylon, be like the sons of Babylon, although by Election and Consolation you are freed.
> Article 8. There are Elect and Consoled in every region of the world... Such are the Good Men of Toulouse, the Poor of Lyon, the Albigenses, those in the neighbourhood of Verona and Bergamo, the Bajolais of Galicia and Tuscany, the Bégards and the Bulgars. By the underground routes you will conduct them to your chapters and to those who feel fear, you will grant the Consolamentum outside the chapters, in front of three witnesses.
> Article 9. You will fraternally receive the Brothers of these groups and moreover the Consoled of Spain and Cyprus will fraternally receive the Saracens, the Druze and those who live in Lebanon. And if the divine Spirit enlivens the Saracens or Druze, you may admit them as Elect or as Consoled.

Articles 13–17 describe the *Ritual of Consolamentum* in which the Preceptor hears the neophyte's confession (normally the prerogative of ordained priests), recites from the Psalms, the antiphon from Deuteronomy, the 'prayer of Moses', *Magnificetur, fortitude, Domini* (Numbers 14: 17–21), and after placing a ring on the right index finger of the brother, the 'prayer of Baphomet', which opens the Koran and bears the name [Al] Fatiha. The brother is anointed on his eyelids and the figure of Baphomet is shown to all present whilst the preceptor speaks the words from Matthew 4:16 (and Isaiah 9:1–12): 'The people who sat in darkness have seen a great light, and for those who sat in the region and shadow of death light has dawned.' (It is possible that these words really were used in a Templar ritual—they have a compelling Manichaean quality and have been set to music not only by Handel in his *Messiah*, but also by Sir John Tavener and dated 13 October.) All the brothers call out 'Yah Allah', kiss the image and touch their belts. The chapter is closed by 'the song taken from the Book of Wisdom' (thought to be the Book of Sirach, or Ecclesiasticus and considered part of the Apocrypha). The question of Baphomet and the statue or 'head' will be considered in a separate chapter. Article 20 states that a Consoled brother may not be chosen as Grand Master.

This summary is in order to give readers a taste of the contents, not to endorse them. In fact they were denounced as a much later forgery by Hans Prutz in *Geheimlehre und Geheimstatuten des Tempelherren-Ordens*, Berlin 1879. This is a very thorough analysis, but has not convinced everyone, René Gilles for example. For instance, according to Prutz, article 9 of the *Book of Baptism by Fire* states: 'You will fraternally receive the Saracens, the Druze and those who live in Lebanon.' The Druze were known to exist but their beliefs were apparently not known in the Middle Ages, neither crusaders nor pilgrims mentioned them. It was not until 1838 when Sylvestre de Sacy published his work *Exposé de la Religion des Druzes* that they became known. (We might add that the designations 'County of Tripoli' and 'Kingdom of Jerusalem' were more usual than 'Lebanon' during the Middle Ages when it was part of the crusader states.) Many of the passages in the articles are distortions of biblical passages, put together into what Prutz calls a vague deistic mosaic. Other passages are almost word for word adaptations from the accounts of the trials—statements that were taken down by scribes in French and then put into Latin. Michelet's *Procès des Templiers*, containing the depositions in Latin, appeared in 1851. The supposed 'secret signs' show many identical features with a work published in Leyden in 1690, and in any case refer to foot positions, handshakes and undone buttons—which would hardly apply to a Templar's habit—familiar to Masonic traditions. Prutz shows furthermore that the articles relating to the heretics of Orléans (Etienne and Lisoë were burnt at the stake for heresy in Orléans in 1022) were almost word for word identical with passages in a history of the heretics of the Middle Ages by Gian Domenico Mansi (1692–1769), an Italian theologian and historian.[96] This material would hardly have been known by Templars in the thirteenth century! We know that history is full of forged documents and here it does seem likely, as Prutz states, that the 'secret statutes' were forged by a particular nineteenth-century Masonic group, perhaps to give themselves a certain authenticity. Prutz points out the similarity of certain expressions with Masonic ones.

What of the names mentioned as signatories of the document? Some are names known to us mainly from the trials' transcripts. It would be very easy, therefore, for a forger to add these names. However, it must be asked why certain knights are mentioned by name in the transcripts as having introduced certain practices into the Order. We will consider these in more detail. Mathieu de Tramlay, named as the scribe of the *Book of the Elect*, has not proved verifiable; his name does not appear in Michelet's *Procès* as a source. Robert de Sandford or Samfort is listed as the Master of the Temple in England from 1229 to 1248.[97] He is mentioned as having received a letter from his friend Guillaume de Sonnac, who was Grand Master of the Order from 1247 to 1250, stating that Guillaume had taken Damietta in Egypt— though he was to die in the second battle. There is no record linking Robert's name with the introduction of unseemly practices, other than in the 'secret statutes'. It is a different matter with the name of 'Master Roncelin', Roncelin (or Roncelinus) de Fos, though being certain of his activities is quite difficult due to the fact that he came from a large Provençal family with property at Fos-sur-Mer and Hyères, and at least one other relative bore the name Roncelin and appears to have been a Templar also.[98] However, genealogies and other documents do record a Roncelin, son of Roger and Tiburgette (née de Baux), born possibly at Bormes, and brother of Philippe, Guillaume and Bellière (also called Sybille or Belette). The de Baux family claimed descent from one of the three Magi, Balthazar, who bears the frankincense.[99] Roncelin was commander at Tortosa (Tartus) in Syria 1241–42, Master in England 1252–56 or 1259 (or 1251–53, according to Parker), and Master in Provence the remainder, until 1278 or 1280, his assumed death. His family is thought to have had Cathar sympathies and were horrified by the massacre of Cathars by Simon de Montfort at Béziers in 1209. Another anti-clerical aspect to him was possible because his family became involved in the power struggle between the papacy and the Holy Roman Empire. Although this took place primarily in Italy with the two parties, Guelphs and Ghibellines, it spilled over into southern France. In 1226 Pons de Fos and Barral de Baux (both part of the large family to which Roncelin belonged) declared their loyalty to the Emperor Frederick II of Hohenstaufen. In Provence, support for the Ghibellines was strong.[100] Julius Evola, though criticized for being rather 'far right', has nonetheless written in an interesting way on the connection between the Grail and the Ghibelline party.[101] Roncelin's name appears on deeds and for receptions in several local records. In the trials' transcripts he is mentioned as having received various brothers into the Order, such as Raymbaud de Caron, interrogated at Chinon in August 1308 (see the 'Chinon Parchment').[102] More significantly, however, in the trial of Geoffrey de Gonneville, Preceptor of Aquitaine and Poitou, Geoffrey states that he had heard it said that evil and perverse practices were introduced into the statutes by 'Master Roncelin' and also by Master Thomas Bérard or Béraud, that the denials of Christ were in memory of the denials of Peter.[103]

Thomas Bérard, who was possibly English, was Grand Master of the Order from 1256 to 1273. In 1252 he was together with Roncelin in Palestine.[104] When the castle of Safed fell to the Egyptian Mameluks in 1266, one story is that he renounced Christianity in order to gain his freedom.[105] This version, however, does not appear in the more reliable histories, but it may be a reason why his name was appended to the statutes. Robert de Samfort, Roncelin de Fos and Thomas Bérard were contemporaries, their names are linked and it is possible that one or all did endorse further practices into the Order. Their service in the Holy Land brought them into contact with Muslims, probably also Sufis, possibly Druze and Nizari Ismailis

('Assassins')—we will look at some of these beliefs and practices later. This does not endorse the 'secret statutes' however. Because Roncelin was accused by Geoffrey de Gonneville, his name has been seized upon by subsequent spurious societies and blamed for corrupting the Order. Stephen of Stapelbridge said in his interrogation that he had heard that the Order's errors had originated in the diocese of Agen[106]—though in Aquitaine, it was part of the Templar holdings which seems to have been under Roncelin's jurisdiction in Provence.[107]

Why might a Masonic-type brotherhood, a possible neo-Templar order, have created the statutes? One purpose may have been to stir up anti-Catholic prejudice and to support a restored Holy Roman Empire, dissolved in 1806, or even to set up a United States of Europe. The double-headed eagle emblem was part of the coat of arms of Holy Roman Emperor Frederick II, and became the 32nd and 33rd badges of the Scottish Rite. It was also the seal of Bertram von Esbeck, Master of the Temple in Germany in 1296.[108] Because the Order was considered so powerful and wealthy, the idea that it may have continued in some form in order to control international politics lingers on (see, for example, Umberto Eco's novel *Foucault's Pendulum*), and finds its way into various conspiracy theories. Apart from being against the Roman Church, the statutes do not put across any overtly political message. Instead the main impression gained is of an attempt to water down Christianity (in spite of mentioning all or some of the prayer of John: 17), to deny Christ as being divine and having passed through death. Although it is important to enjoy mutual good understanding with people of other faiths, it does not mean that we should subscribe to a mish-mash of vague religious beliefs and practices drawn from everywhere. The Templars no doubt learned much from their meetings with people following other paths, and they were exhorted to seek out the excommunicated, but this does not mean that they *really* denied Christianity. Individual brothers may have suffered doubts, it is only natural. But, as a whole, the aim of the Order was to practise a widened Christianity, to prepare for a future Christianity, which could include certain so-called heresies and pre-Christian wisdom.

9. The Head and Baphomet

Item, that in each province they had idols, namely heads, of which some had three faces, and some one, and others had a human skull.
Item, that they adored these idols or that idol, and especially in their great chapters and assemblies.[109]

... a man's head with a large beard, which head they kiss and worship at all their provincial chapters, but this is not all the brothers know, save only the Grand Master and the old ones. [*Philip's instructions to his seneschals*]

Brother Pierre d'Arbley suspected that the 'idol' had two faces, and his kinsman Guillaume d'Arbley made the point that the 'idol' itself, as distinct from copies, was exhibited at general chapters, implying that it was only shown to senior members of the Order on special occasions.

The treasurer of the Paris Temple, Jean de Turn, spoke of a painted head in the form of a picture, which he had adored at one of these chapters.

... about the natural size of a man's head, with a very fierce-looking face and beard. [*Deposition of Jean Taillefer*][110]

The most graphic description came from a loquacious serving brother called Raoul de Gizy. He had seen the head in seven different chapters, some of which had been held by Hugues de Pairaud, the Visitor. When it was shown, all those present prostrated themselves on the ground and worshipped it. It had a terrible appearance, seeming to be a figure of a demon, called in French *un maufé*. Whenever he saw it, he was filled with fear and he could scarcely look at it without trembling. However he had never worshipped it in his heart.[111]

[*Etienne de Troyes at Poitiers*]: ... at the prime of the night they brought a head, a priest carrying it, preceded by two brothers with two large wax candles upon a silver candelabra, and he [the priest] put it upon the altar on two cushions on a certain tapestry of silk, and the head was as it seemed to him, flesh from the crown to the nape of the neck, indeed a face of flesh, and it seemed to him very bluish in colour and stained, with a beard having a mixture of white and black hairs similar to the beards of some Templars. And then the Visitor [Hugues de Pairaud] stood up, saying to all: 'We must proceed, adore it and make homage to it, which helps us and does not abandon us,' and then all went with great reverence and made homage to it and adored that head. And this witness who heard it said that it was the head of the first Master of the Order, namely Brother Hugues de Payns. And from the nape of the neck to the shoulders it was completely encrusted with precious stones of gold and silver.[112]

Brother John de Donyngton, of the Order of the Minorites ... deposed that some years back an old veteran of the Temple (whose name he could not recollect) told him that the Order possessed four chief idols in England, one at London in the sacristy of the Temple; another at the preceptory of Bistele-sham; a third at Bruere in Lincolnshire; and the fourth in some place beyond the Humber ... that Brother William de la More, the Master of the Temple, introduced the melancholy idolatry of the Templars into England, and brought with him a great roll, whereon were inscribed in large characters the wicked practices and observances of the Order. The said old veteran also told the deponent that many of the Templars carried idols about with them in boxes, etc. etc.[113]

In this last example, it becomes William de la More who is accused of corrupting the Order. As he was the last Master of the English Temple, 1298–1312, it seems likely there was a confusion between him and one of the aforementioned Masters. This witness, moreover, was unlikely to have been mistreated, as he was not a Templar but a member of the Franciscan Order (Order of

Friars Minor, or Minorite Friars). We see that the description of the head varied considerably—it was fleshlike or it was gilded, fearful, wooden or painted, but all state it was bearded. It was probably not shown to all, even though some witnesses mention seeing it in several chapters.

In some cases the head was called, or identified with, Baphomet:

> Other Templars questioned after Jean de Cassagne had seen, variously, an idol like a bearded head which was the figure of Baphomet, a figure called Yalla (a Saracen word), a black and white idol, and a wooden idol.[114]

This was also the case in the 'secret statutes', as we saw in article 17 of the *Baptism of Fire*. One's first reaction may be that these were further monstrous accusations brought about by the evil effects of torture. But in fact, as we shall see, there is much more to this claim than mere idolatry and we are led into the more mysterious realms of dualism and to the experiences at the threshold of the spiritual world. Rudolf Steiner continues in his short description of the Templar rituals:

> At the outset, the Templars were in a position as if they had adjured the cross. After all of this had been made clear to the Templar, he was shown a symbolical figure of the Divine Being in the form of a venerable man with a long beard (symbolizing the Father).[115]

To come to a clearer understanding of what the knights may have experienced, we will consider what may take place when we come to the threshold of the spiritual world, where we cross into a state in which spiritual beings can approach us. We can have the experience of its Guardian, an entity that is really a wise guide but who initially can appear to us in the guise of our own double—a fearful image of all that we still have to overcome in ourselves.

> A thoroughly horrid, ghostly being stands before us. Hence we shall need full presence of mind and complete confidence in the safety and reliability of our cognitive path... The Guar-

dian then reveals the meaning of this moment in words, somewhat as follows: '... Now, however, all the good and bad aspects of your past lives are to be revealed to you. You will see them for yourself. They have been interwoven with your being all along... They are assuming an independent form... I am that selfsame being, who made a body for itself out of your good and wicked deeds... Now that I have come forth from you, this hidden wisdom has also left you and will take care of you no longer. Instead it puts the work into your own hands. I myself, if I am not to fall into corruption, must become a perfect and glorious being... My being will be changed and become radiantly beautiful only when you have made amends for all your wrongs and so purified yourself that you become incapable of further evil...'

The Guardian's function is to warn us not to go further unless we feel strong enough to meet the challenges contained in the words addressed to us. Horrid as it may be, the Guardian's appearance is, after all, but the consequence of our own past lives.[116]

Concealed within you is a vigilant being, who keeps careful, solicitous watch over the border that you must cross when entering the suprasensory world. This spiritual being within you is you yourself. Your ordinary consciousness can no more recognize it than the eye can see itself. It is the 'Guardian of the Threshold' of the spiritual world. When you experience the sense that you are not only that being, but also *outside* that being, *facing* it—in that moment you recognize the 'Guardian.'[117]

In spiritual training we are warned not to attempt to progress further until we have come to accept this Guardian. But as we make progress, we will attain a further experience, of a magnificent form:

The beauty of this form is difficult to describe in ordinary language ... the great Guardian of the Threshold announces his presence soon after the meeting with the first Guardian ...

The second Guardian of the Threshold emits an indescribable radiance. Union with this Guardian is a distant goal for the beholding soul. Yet the certainty is also present that such a union is possible only after all the powers that have flowed into us from this world have been expended in the service of liberating and redeeming it.[118]

In the language of Imagination Steiner thus describes these encounters with beings that are part of us and yet also beyond us, leading to our divine higher self that can unite with Christ. Probably the head was not intended to represent aspects of the Templars' own selves, but the effect it could have was—doubtless because of the ritual involved—one of revealing the dual 'Guardian' nature. Their spiritual life was not a modern initiatory path such as we have today in anthroposophy, but some of the knights did experience a Christian-Gnostic initiation such as Steiner has described. Even if this was not a fully developed attainment there was still a loosening of the subtler sheaths. Medieval mystics and contemplatives were often plagued by visions of demonic forms. Such visions could easily have been projected onto the image of the head. Whether what should have been a spiritual practice for just a few brothers became more general and was misunderstood, is hard to say. Pietzner offers the following explanation for the experience:

> Finally the seventh step was the revealing of the so-called idol, of the Baphomet, or, as he was also called, of 'Himself' . . . If the initiate had been able to go through the six steps including the anointing of his eyes to cleanse and purify his sight, he was now able to *see* what was shown to him. For some it was the revelation of the head of a bearded man, a beautiful head (as Rudolf Steiner called it) . . . But for those who were able, after the six steps, to maintain their consciousness fully for the seventh step, the true head of the Baphomet was revealed, and for a moment there appeared to them on a silver platter the head of John the Baptist. The black grail was shown as the deepest expression of the counterforces which the Templar himself would have to face.[119]

There were claims made by a number of churches in medieval Europe that they held the head of John the Baptist. Head-shaped reliquaries were not unusual for holding alleged relics, and one suggestion is that some of the heads the knights saw were these. But in connection with the bleeding head which Pietzner believed could appear to the knights, this would be a warning of the 'double' forces to be overcome in oneself and of evil forces outside, as a bleeding head on a platter was, according to Steiner, a symbol of black magic:

> In other parts of Europe the mysteries fell into decadence and were then made profane in a disgusting, repulsive manner. Their symbol of offering was a dish in which a bleeding head was placed. It was thought that something might be aroused in a human being on seeing this head. It was black magic that was being performed, the opposite of the mystery of the Holy Grail.[120]

There is no suggestion that the knights were *really* shown a bleeding head—it was an inner, visionary experience that could occur, as already stated, in which the head appeared as fearful or evil. Intended to reveal the wisdom of the divine Father, as we shall show more clearly later on, it could bring about in the knight an experience of the adversary forces' power in attempting to drag him down. First he would see what remained in himself that still had to be overcome, and then he would be led on to the experience of the head in its 'beautiful' aspect.[120a]

The meaning of Baphomet

We can gain a better understanding of this by considering who or what Baphomet really is. Some historians have said that the name was a misinterpretation of Mahomet or Mohammed. This sounds too simplistic, but there is evidence that there was a corruption or confusion of names. Historian Helen Nicholson has provided a translation of a poem by Ricaut Bonomel, a brother serving in the Holy Land in 1265 or 1266. In the whole poem his despair is very evident:

> Then whoever fights the Turks is a real fool since Jesus Christ certainly does not attack them;
> They have conquered and will conquer, it grieves me to say, Franks, Tartars, Armenians and Persians.
> And we are defeated every day for God sleeps, who used to stand watch, and
> Bafometz [Mohammed] acts with all his power and spurs on Melicadefer [Baibars, the Turkish leader].[121]

The Spanish poem *el Poema del Mio Cid* of 1140 has another version of the name:

> Los moros llaman Mafomat
> E los Cristianos Santi Yague (v. 73)

> The Moors shout Mohammed
> And the Christians shout Saint James.[122]

A confusion of names was partly true in the Middle Ages, but there is no intention of implying that the prophet Mohammed is to be identified with veneration of an 'idol'. To the brothers, the Saracens were the 'enemy' because they were capturing the Holy Land, less so because they were of a different faith. They often pursued good relations with them (to their own detriment, as they were accused of too much fraternization), and sometimes defended them against the zeal of the more simple-minded crusaders.

One often quoted explanation of the name is that it is a corruption of the Greek *Baphe metis*, meaning 'baptism of wisdom'. Hugh Schonfield in *The Essene Odyssey*,[123] by using the 'Atbash cipher'—substituting letters of the Hebrew alphabet—arrives at 'Sophia' or 'wisdom', an interpretation popularized by Dan Brown's *Da Vinci Code*. Eliphas Lévi likened the figure to the symbol of ultimate wisdom *Azoth,* connected to the Philosophers' Stone, and stated it to be also the Egyptian goat-god, Mendes—from which he suggests arose the familiar Tarot card image of the 'devil'.[124] But the Sufi teacher Idries Shah gives one of the fullest explanations:

... Western scholars have recently supposed that 'Baphomet' has no connection with Mohammed, but could well be a corruption of the Arabic *abufihamat* (pronounced in Moorish Spanish something like *bufihimat*). The word means 'father of understanding'. In Arabic, 'father' is taken to mean 'source, chief seat of', and so on. In Sufi terminology, *ras el-fahmat* (head of knowledge) means the mentation of man after undergoing refinement—the transmuted consciousness.

It will be noted that the word 'knowledge, understanding' used here is derived from the Arabic FHM root. FHM, in turn, is used to stand both for FHM and derivatives, meaning 'knowledge' ... and [also] for 'black, coalman' and so on.

The Baphomet is none other than the symbol of the completed man. The black head, negro head, or Turk's head which appears in heraldry and in English country-inn signs is a crusader substitute word (cant word) for this kind of knowledge.

It may be noted that the shield of Hugues de Payen, the founder (with Bisol de St Omer) of the Templars in AD 1118, carried three black human heads—the heads of knowledge.

The use of this term, especially the 'wondrous head' theme, recurs throughout medieval history. Pope Gerbert (Silvester II) who studied in Moorish Spain, is stated to have made a brazen head ... Albertus Magnus spent thirty years making his marvellous brass head. Thomas Aquinas, pupil at the time to Albertus, smashed the head, which 'talked too much' ... This artificial head is not made of brass. Artificial it is, in that it is the product of 'work' in the Sufic sense. Ultimately, of course, it is the head of the individual himself ... In Arabic, 'brass' is spelled SuFR, connected with the concept of 'yellowness'. The 'head of brass' is a rhyming homonym for 'head of gold', which is spelled in exactly the same way. The Golden Head is a Sufi phrase used to refer to a person whose inner consciousness has been 'transmuted into gold' by means of Sufic study and activity...

The phrase, 'I am making a head', used by dervishes to indicate their Sufic dedication in certain exercises, could very well have been used by Albertus Magnus, or Pope Silvester, and transmitted in the literal sense, believed to refer to some sort of artefact.[125]

Most interesting ideas are contained here—including the meaning of the popularity of 'Turk's head' signs and images, but did the knights know they were 'making a head'? However, there is still a *dual* nature of good and evil to Baphomet. Rudolf Steiner was asked by a teacher from the first Waldorf School in Stuttgart what 'Baphomet' meant. He replied:

Baphomet is a being of the ahrimanic world who appears to people when they are being tortured. That happens really cleverly, since they bring a lot of visions back with them when they return to consciousness.[126]

A 'head of wisdom' *and* an ahrimanic being—how can we reconcile this? One possible way of explaining it is recalling that thoughts create elemental beings:

...we perceive that behind the thoughts, which on the physical plane were mere shadow images, lies something which is alive and that the world of thought is full of life and activity. We become aware that in truth a host of elemental spirits is spreading out behind it...[127]

To a certain extent, some Templars must have thought of Islam as something to be overcome, and thereby created a 'thought' entity, which attracted the 'hate entity' of the more ordinary crusaders and became an 'egregore'—a magical entity created by focused thoughts of a negative, bigoted kind. In spite of fraternization, there must have occurred this aspect also, especially in the heat of battle. Thus, under torture and conditions of extreme hardship, the 'head of wisdom' took on a 'double' aspect (related to the previously described threshold experiences) and appeared in the guise of an egregore composed of what the Templars thought they were fighting against in Islam—there may have been an awareness of the genuine Sufi teaching of the 'abufihamat', but this became turned into the opposite, the idol Baphomet.

Before considering the true nature of the head of wisdom let us explore some 'heads' and head cults in general. Firstly, have any heads been discovered in Templar properties? Not apparently in the forms described in the trials, but a search in the Paris Temple did reveal 'a certain large beautiful silver-gilt head, shaped like that of a woman, within which were the bones of a single head . . . and the said bones were considered as similar to the bones of the head of a small woman, and it was said by some that it was the head of one of the eleven thousand virgins.'[128] Such treasured relics were commonplace in medieval times and often kept in a reliquary fashioned like a head. Thus confusion wrought by torture could have led brothers to suppose that they had venerated what was in fact a casket of relics. However, there are a few other interesting representations extant. At Templecombe in Somerset, on the site of a former preceptory, a strange painted wooden panel was discovered during restoration of an old house near the church and is now on display in the church itself. It

Painted medieval wooden panel from Templecombe church, Somerset

Carved Romanesque wooden head found in Cameley church, Somerset

shows a fine bearded human countenance and definitely bears a distinctive quality. Is it a representation of Christ—or was it an image used in specific rituals? More recently another head was found in Somerset, at Cameley Church, once apparently a Templar possession, a carved wooden relief of a man's head with a forked beard. At the back are nine indented squares which may have held relics.[129] Though not as fine as the Templecombe image, it is a possible contender for a ritual object. Further suggestions have been made that the image of the Turin shroud was also used by the Templars, as for a time it was in the hands of the family of Geoffrey de Charney, a brother burned at the stake in Paris with Jacques de Molay in 1314. Though this could of course have simply been a position of safe keeping for what was held to be such a holy relic. These images, like the descriptions, are always bearded, and it is interesting that the Templars were required to grow beards and not be clean-shaven like other monks. That this was perhaps more convenient when in battle is too simplistic—most armies do not sport beards.

Carved heads are common emblems in medieval churches, both Templar—such as the wonderful grotesque faces in the London Temple Church—and in many other non-Templar ones, so we must be cautious in not ascribing every head to be a special ritual object.

A sacred head cult was common to the Celts, who sometimes kept mummified heads of their enemies, not just as trophies but in order to acquire something of their forces. Many stone head images have been found in Celtic sites and can still be seen carved above some holy wells. Legends of miraculous heads—sometimes being restored to their owner—were also associated with healing springs, such as St Winifred's in Wales.

Oracular heads which apparently 'spoke' also captured the popular medieval imagination. We have heard about the one created by Albertus Magnus, which Thomas Aquinas disliked and smashed one day. Friar Roger Bacon and the cleric Robert Grosseteste also were said to have devised talking brass heads. How these came to be made to speak is not clear, whether it was by ventriloquism or by a magical act that imbued them with elemental beings, or whether discarnate entities were working through a human medium is uncertain, but such objects date back to the ancient magical practices of the Egyptians, and also the *teraphim* used in Babylonia, as Emil Bock cites:

> Many have puzzled over what was meant by Laban's *teraphim*, which Rachel purloined. There are many gruesome descriptions of *teraphim* from later centuries that were in use in decadent Babylonia. Heads of slain children, mostly first-born males, were set up somewhere with gilded lips, and by a number of sinister invocation-charms were made to speak. In regard to the more ancient times and the cults that had not yet fallen into decadence, the remark of the *Sepher Hayashar* is probably an indication: 'Some make *teraphim* in the form of a man out of gold and silver, and at certain hours this figure receives the forces of the constellations and predicts the future.' (Chvol'son, *Die Ssabier,* Vol. II).[130]

We can begin to understand how the Templars' accusers associated these mysterious magic heads with 'peculiar practices' of the Order.

Heads appear in the Grail legends too. In the thirteenth century story *The High Book of the Grail (Perlevaus)*, three mysterious maidens appear at the court of King Arthur with a cart. One of them takes off her headdress and speaks:

> ... I had a beautiful head of hair, all braided with rich golden tresses, until the knight came to the house of the Fisher King; because he failed to ask the question I am now bald, and my hair will not return until a knight goes and asks the question more properly, or goes and conquers the Grail. But sire, you

have not yet seen the great harm that this has wrought. Outside this hall there is a cart pulled by three white stags . . . The
cart is draped in black samite, with a gold cross on top as long
as the cart itself. And on the cart beneath the drape are the
heads of 150 knights, some sealed in gold, some in silver, and
others in lead. And the rich Fisher King wants you to know
that this calamity is all the fault of the knight who did not ask
who was served from the Grail.[131]

In this story the failure to ask the Grail question has resulted in a
further misfortune—a maiden has lost all her hair and the deaths
of a king and queen and 150 knights has occurred, as a priest
explains to Gawain:

'In faith,' said Sir Gawain, 'I am greatly puzzled about three
maidens who came to the court of King Arthur, bearing two
heads—the head of a king and the head of a queen, and in a
cart they were carrying the heads of 150 knights . . .'
    'Indeed,' said the priest, 'but the maidens said that by the
queen the king was betrayed and killed, along with the knights
whose heads were in the cart. She spoke true, as Josephus tells
us; for he reminds us that by Eve was Adam betrayed, and all
the people who have lived since, and the ages to come will
always suffer for it. Because Adam was the first man, he is
called king, for he was our earthly father, and his wife is
queen. And the heads of the knights sealed in gold signify the
New Law, and the heads sealed in silver the Jews, and the
heads sealed in lead the false law of the Saracens. Of these
three kinds of men is the world composed.'[132]

Not only should Parzival's question win him the Grail kingship,
but also it evidently reverses the 'Fall'. Or rather it is the Holy
Blood carried in the heart which does so—the blood which unites
etherically with Christ's. Heart-based thinking must replace
mummified 'head' thinking. In a continuation of Chrétien de
Troyes' *Perceval*, there is an intriguing interpolation:

Nicodemus had carved and fashioned a head in the likeness of
the Lord on the day that he had seen Him on the cross. But of

this I am sure, that the Lord God set His Hand to the shaping of it, as they say; for no man ever saw one like it nor could it be made by human hands. Most of you who have been at Lucca know it and have seen it.[133]

This is the Holy Face of Lucca (*Volto Santo di Lucca*), in the cathedral of San Martino. Lucca also contained a Templar preceptory, though the image was presented much earlier than the Templar time in AD 742—except that the present image is a thirteenth-century copy of the original. Nicodemus, who came to Christ 'by night'—for initiation purposes—and assisted Joseph of Arimathaea in taking down Christ's body from the cross, was, according to Sergei Prokofieff, a reincarnated pupil of the initiate Scythianos, together with Joseph.[134] Scythianos' mission was to penetrate the secrets of the physical body and how it was created by the highest spiritual beings. A realm of possibilities that will one day result in human beings achieving the power to transform its forces and develop the 'phantom' or 'resurrection body' is hinted at in these accounts. Thus we have come some way from the varied and interpenetrating meanings of the head of the Templars to one of the highest mysteries.

10. The Wisdom of the Zohar

It is being put forward here, that for our purposes the real source
of the 'head of wisdom' is to be found in the Jewish esoteric
teachings of the Kabbalah, in particular the *Zohar*. The *Book of
Splendour* or *Zohar* is thought to have been written down in the
thirteenth century, possibly in Girona, Spain by Moses ben
Shem-Tov de Leon, but some scholars think it comprises a much
earlier, oral teaching. Jewish mysticism flourished in medieval
times in such centres as Girona or Narbonne in France.[135]
Christian figures such as Ramon Lull (or Lully, 1232–1314) of
Majorca were certainly influenced by it and Lull had contacts
with the Templars. But it is very likely that there were oppor-
tunities for imbibing the wisdom of the Kabbalah well before
then. At an early stage in its history the Order chose Psalm 133
as its special Psalm, and it was recited by the chaplain at a
normal reception of a brother:[136]

1. Behold, how good and pleasant it is
    when brothers dwell in unity!
2. It is like the precious oil upon the head,
    running down upon the beard,
    upon the beard of Aaron,
    running down on the collar of his robes!
3. It is like the dew of Hermon,
    which falls on the mountains of Zion!
    For there the Lord has commanded the blessing,
    Life for evermore.   (RSV)

At first glance it might seem simply to be extolling the virtues of
a communal life of brotherhood, acknowledging Aaron as the
first head of the Hebrew high priesthood, anointed by Moses,
and therefore a prototype for all priests in the Judaeo-Christian
tradition. It also refers to Mount Hermon, the sacred mountain
or 'forbidden place' (Aramaic), which marked the northern
limits of Israel's conquests. With its truncated cone divided into
three summits, its snowy whiteness reflected in the Sea of

Galilee, it was, and no doubt still is, a beloved symbol of the 'high place' where one holy enough might walk with the Lord. Its melting snows are the main source of the River Jordan. Sometimes also called Mount Zion it is therefore a further symbol of the Christ mystery and the New Jerusalem.

Like much of the Bible, however, this Psalm contains a hidden meaning which in this case is revealed by the *Zohar*, which consists of several books describing the teachings passed on by Rabbi Simeon ben-Yochai. It describes a head, the *Macroprosopus* or Vast Countenance, proceeding from the *Ain Soph*, the infinite and limitless one. This most ancient head is perceived as creating a shadow image of itself, the *Microprosopus* or Lesser Countenance, which becomes the Creation or Microcosm. Eliphas Lévi gives us a rather beautiful paraphrase:

> Thus, when God had permitted the night to exist, in order that the stars might appear, he turned towards the shadow he had made and considered it, to give it a face.
>
> He formed an image on the veil with which he had covered his glory, and this image smiled at him, and he regarded this image as his own, so that he might create man in accordance with it ...
>
> The divine image is a double one. There are the heads of light and of shadow, the white ideal and the black ideal, the upper head and the lower. One is the dream of the Man-God, the other is the invention of the God-Man. One represents the God of the wise, and the other, the idol of the lowly.
>
> All light, in truth, implies shadow and possesses its brilliance only in opposition to that shadow.
>
> The luminous head pours out upon the dark one a constant dew of splendour.
>
> 'Let me in, my beloved,' says God to intelligence, 'for my head is filled with dew, and among the curls of my hair wander the tears of night.'
>
> This dew is the manna by which the souls of the just are nourished. The elect are hungry for it and gather it abundantly in the fields of heaven.

These drops are round pearls, brilliant as diamonds and clear as crystal.

They are white and glow with all colours, for there is one simple truth alone: the splendour of all things...[137]

Although something of dualism is implied here, the shadow head or microcosm, which also becomes man, is not created by an evil being as in some Gnostic systems, but by the Godhead as a reflection of itself.

From *The Kabbalah Unveiled,* translated by S.L. MacGregor Mathers (of *Golden Dawn* fame) from a Latin version of the *Zohar* called the *Kabbala Denudata,* we will look at a few extracts to give us further understanding. (The notes in brackets are by MacGregor Mathers).[138]

From *The Book of Concealed Mystery*:

4. Until that head (which is incomprehensible) desired by all desires (proceeding from AIN SVP, *Ain Soph,* the infinite and limitless one), appeared and communicated the vestments of honour.

9. The head which is incomprehensible is secret in secret. [This head is Macroprosopus, the Vast Countenance, and is the same as the Ancient One, or Crown Kether. It is secret, for therein are hidden the other potentialities.]

10. But it hath been formed and prepared in the likeness of a cranium, and is filled with the crystalline dew.

From *The Greater Holy Assembly*:

Chapter 3: Concerning the Ancient One
39. White are His garments, and His appearance is the likeness of a Face vast and terrible.

Chapter 4: Concerning the dew
44. And from that skull distillith a dew upon Him which is external, and filleth His head daily.

45. And from that dew which floweth down from His head, that (*namely*) which is external, the dead are raised up in the world to come.

Chapter 5: Further concerning the skull

54. And He Himself, the Most Ancient of the Most Ancient
Ones, is called ARIK DANPIN, *Arikh Da-Anpin*, the Vast
Countenance, or Macroprosopus; and He Who is more
external is called ZOIR ANPIN, *Zauir Anpin*, or Him Who
hath the Lesser Countenance (*Microprosopus*), in opposition
to the Ancient Eternal Holy One, the Holy of the Holy
Ones.

Chapter 11, Concerning the Beard of Macroprosopus in general

211. The beard, whose hairs hang down even unto the breast,
white as snow; the adornment of adornments, the conceal-
ment of concealments, the truth of all truths.

213. That is the beard of adornment, true and perfect, from
which flow down thirteen fountains, scattering the most
precious balm of splendour.

214. This is disposed in thirteen forms.

229. Through those thirteen dispositions do they flow down,
and the thirteen fountains of precious oil issue forth, and they
flow down through all those inferiors, and in that oil do they
shine, and with that oil are they anointed.

245. Therefore it is said: Wisdom will cry without when She
passeth from the concealed brain of Macroprosopus unto the
brain of Microprosopus, through those longer hairs; and thus
as it were extrinsically those two brains are connected and
become in this way one brain.

Chapter 12 Concerning the Beard of Macroprosopus

319. But what beard is manifested? The beard of the Great
High Priest, and from that beard descendeth the influx unto
the inferior beard of the inferior high priest [*the Great High
Priest is the son, Microprosopus, symbolized on earth by the
High Priest. Compare what St. Paul says about Christ being our
Great High Priest.*]

320. How is the beard of the high priest disposed? The beard
of the high priest is disposed in eight conformations. Because
also the high priest hath eight vestments, when the ointment
descendeth upon his beard.

321. This is that which is written, Ps. 133, ii: 'Like the precious oil upon the head descending upon the beard, the beard of Aaron, which descendeth according to the proportion of his attributes,' etc.

322. And whence is this to us? Because it is written in the same place: 'Also for brethren to dwell together in equality.' The word 'also' increaseth the signification of the inferior high priest.

Chapter 27 Concerning the skull of Microprosopus
536. This is the tradition. When the White Head [*another title for the Crown, Kether*] propounded unto Himself to superadd ornament unto his own adornment, He constituted, prepared, and produced one single spark from His intense splendour of light. He fanned it and condensed it (or conformed it).

546. In that skull distilleth the dew [*this subtle air, fire and dew are analogous to the 3 'mother letters' of the Sepher Yetzirah, A, M, and SH, the letter A symbolizing air, the medium between M the water and SH the fire.*]

548. But whensoever it remaineth in that head of Microprosopus, there appeareth in it a redness, like as in crystal, which is white, and there appeareth a red colour in the white colour.

553. And that dew, which distilleth, distilleth daily upon the field of apples, in colour white and red.

Chapter 34 Concerning the beard of Microprosopus
753. We have learned this. There is a descent from the beard which is venerable, holy, excellent, hidden and concealed in all (*the beard namely of Macroprosopus*), through the holy magnificent oil, into the beard of Microprosopus.

758. And when the venerable beard of the Ancient of the Ancient Ones shineth upon this beard of Microprosopus, then the 13 fountains of excellent oil flow down upon this beard.

759. And therein are found 22 parts, and thence extend the 22 letters of the holy law.

From The Lesser Holy Assembly

Chapter 2 Concerning the skull of the ancient one
53. And from this convexity of the joining together of this White Skull daily distilleth a dew into Microprosopus, into that place which is called Heaven; and in that very place shall the dead be raised to life in the time to come.
58. The beginning of that Supernal Wisdom which also is itself the Head, is hidden therein, and is called the Supernal Brain, the Hidden Brain, the Tranquil and Calm Brain; neither doth any man know save He Himself.
59. Three Heads have been formed forth, one within the other, and the other above the other.
60. One head is the Concealed Wisdom, which is covered and is not disclosed.
61. And this Hidden Wisdom is the Head of all things, and the Head of the remaining wisdoms.

Chapter 7 Concerning the brain and the wisdom in general
169. For since this Head is the supreme of all the supernals, hence He is only symbolized as a head alone without body, for the purpose of establishing all things.

Chapter 18. Concerning the beard of Microprosopus
677. In this beard (*of Microprosopus*) floweth down the oil of dignity from the Concealed Ancient One, as it is said, Ps.133, ii: 'Like the excellent oil upon the head, descending upon the beard, the beard of Aaron.'

Thus the deeper significance of Psalm 133 becomes clear and is actually mentioned in the *Zohar*. Furthermore we find many references to this bearded head of wisdom that is perceived as ancient, mighty, vast and terrible, also having three heads or faces. We find the colours white and red mentioned as a significant manifestation of the dew, bringing to mind the white habits of the Templars with their red crosses.

Today it is harder and also less appropriate to reach through to spiritual wisdom by means of symbolism, but in the Middle Ages it was still possible. In earlier times dew was not simply seen as a condensation of water but was understood as a divine substance, which from spiritual science we learn conveys the pure forces of the 'chemical' or 'sound' ether—the forming etheric force of water. This force can be imagined as not having 'fallen' or become weakened by perverted human use, but had, together with the life ether, been protected and held back from man's free use. In German, dew is *Tau*, echoing the ancient concept of the Tao or Great Spirit; in Latin the word is *ros*, from which *Rosicrucian* possibly derives. A beautiful fifteenth-century carol, 'The Holy Boy', refers to Jesus descending to Mary 'like the dew':

> He came all so still
> There his mother was
> Like dew in April
> That falleth on the grass...

The Jesus of St Luke's Gospel bore these unfallen forces in his etheric body and was thus able to receive the Word—the Christ—into it.[139]

The *Zohar* reveals a whole realm of wisdom that was understood in earlier esoteric circles. The more familiar teaching of the ten Sephiroth is of course part of this Kabbalistic wisdom and may have been known to the Templars also. If *Kether* stands for the 'Ancient One', then nine follow—the nine founding knights of the Order. In its Old Testament guise, it reveals a common source of wisdom that can unite Christians, Jews and Muslims. It should be clear now how this mighty teaching was conveyed by means of a symbolic bearded head, carved or painted, shown at some point in a ritual, but its true meaning became completely distorted, confused, dishonoured and maligned by the intervention of adversary forces.

The wisdom of the head has, moreover, a certain connection with the Holy Land itself. The rocky desert region of Judaea, in which Jerusalem stands, can be likened to the 'head' or 'salt pole' of a human being, in which forces die—but release consciousness and the ability to think.[140] In this desert landscape the mightiest consciousness incarnated and passed through death to release the most tremendous life forces of the 'Resurrection Body', as indeed the *Zohar* foretells. Golgotha means 'place of a skull'.

11. Middle Eastern Beliefs:
Nizari Ismailis, Sufis, Druze

Nizari Ismailis

We have shown the remarkable influence of Kabbalistic teachings on the Order, but it is often stated that the Templars came under the influence of some branches of Islam whilst in the Holy Land. One of the most quoted are the Nizari Ismailis, often referred to in the Middle Ages as the Order of Assassins, *Hashshashin*. The Nizari Ismailis are really a branch of Shi'a Islam who place a strong emphasis on social justice and human reason within the mystical Islamic tradition, flourishing today under their leader, the Aga Khan IV, the 49th Imam. In the Middle Ages they occupied mountain fortresses under the leadership of Hassan-I-Sabbah, sometimes called the 'Old Man of the Mountains'. They were said to consume hashish before carrying out political assassinations, promising a glorious vision of paradise to their followers—hence the name. This comes chiefly from an account by Marco Polo who visited a hidden valley of theirs in 1271. They had political dealing with the Templars in that the latter extracted tribute money from them at one stage, and no doubt there were local contacts in the Holy Land, but whether the Templars really imbibed any of their teachings directly seems somewhat unlikely. However, the nine degrees of wisdom that are said to be their initiation are interesting:[141]

In the first degree the seeker took an oath and was taught that the Koran has a superior esoteric meaning.
In the second, the seeker was expected to accept the error of Sunni teaching. He must also hold back his own interpretation of the truth in favour of the Imam's teaching or his direct representative. Imams were considered divinely inspired.
In the third, the seeker was taught Kabbalistic mysteries of seven

and that there were seven divine Ismaili teachers (the wider Shi'ite community recognizes twelve). Their esoteric names and secret words were revealed to him.

In the fourth, he learnt of the seven prophets, Adam, Noah, Abraham, Moses, Jesus, Mohammed and Ismail, and seven mystical helpers, Seth, Shem, Ishmael, Aaron, Simon, Ali and Mohammed, son of Ismail.

In the fifth, the mysteries of twelve were taught—the zodiac, twelve tribes of Israel, and practical magical use of Kabbalistic knowledge. Also twelve 'apostles' were described. Further emphasis of esoteric interpretations of the Koran were also stressed.

In the sixth, there were only the most advanced pupils, as they were taught to abandon the usual Muslim observances, including prayer, fasting and pilgrimage. Philosophical teachings of Pythagoras, Plato and Aristotle were introduced.

In the seventh, the few admitted passed from philosophy to mysticism. The 'Great Secret' was revealed—that all humanity and all creation were one and every single thing was part of a whole. The 'Lord of Time' came mysteriously to awaken the individual's inner power.

In the eighth, the pupil was shown that all exoteric religion and philosophy was superfluous. 'God' became formless, nameless and unknowable.

In the ninth, even 'belief' vanished. The pupil learnt Gnostic teachings, was a 'knower' and a law unto himself. It assumed the surrender of the ego to the divine to the extent that the initiate can now truly act out of his own higher self.

Although not obviously mirrored in Templar teachings, there are, however, parallels in that the seeker learns to turn the accepted religious practice 'on its head' in order to perceive the deeper truths. He may perform actions which the uninitiated consider shocking or refrain from practices believed by the majority to be necessary for salvation. If contacts on a more spiritual level did take place, the brothers serving in the Holy Land might possibly have been inspired and encouraged to develop 'unusual' practices of their own in order to arrive at a greater wisdom. There are also similarities to other initiatory systems. Although the number nine may have appealed to the Order—the so-called Lévitikon taught nine grades of ascent, but seven was the number for the Christian initiation path.

Sufism

In Sufism the emphasis is much more on the inner mystical path than on an accepted religious structure or code of practice and belief. The Sufi master teaches through stories, poetry, design, architecture. Many of the great Sufi poets and teachers were contemporaneous with the Order's time on earth, and the original knights were granted the octagonal Dome of the Rock in Jerusalem which was built in the seventh century on a Sufi mathematical design.[142] But whether the influences extend as far as Idries Shah would have them is open to question. In Sufi poetry the language is romantic and full of yearning, in order to open the heart and connect to the divine and to one's inner divine self. We find a similar conundrum with the mystical language of the Song of Solomon, for which St Bernard of Clairvaux gave a commentary. Whether the brothers could receive wisdom in this form without it disturbing their vow of chastity is another question. Perhaps it was more possible to live in that language in those times, without it seeming as erotic as it appears today. Sufism offered—and still does—an inner 'heart' path that is more akin to the medieval Christian mystics such as Meister Eckhart. Perhaps any influence on the Templars would have been of a more personal kind, rather than on the Order as a whole.

Whilst brothers in the Middle Ages may have toyed with Islamic mysticism, we should remember that in Europe the Dominican Order, and especially Thomas Aquinas in the thirteenth century, was teaching the importance of *individual* thinking and warning against the danger of becoming absorbed into a 'cosmic all' such as was taught by mystical Islam and other more eastern inspired paths, and of losing this precious gift which the spiritual world wanted to bestow.[143]

The Druze, or *Mowahhidoon* (*monotheistic*)[144]

We mentioned the Druze briefly when discussing the 'secret statutes. They were barely known until the eighteenth or nineteenth centuries, due to their secrecy in guarding their rites and beliefs. Today, roughly 900,000–1,300,000 live in Lebanon, Syria, Israel, Jordan and also in the western world. Basically they are an offshoot of Islam, but their theology is called *hikma* and they believe in an incarnation of God in the Fatimid Caliph al-Hakim who disappeared in 1021—there were nine previous 'manifestations'. This 'incarnational heresy' (according to traditional Islam) is sometimes blamed on Christian influences. But Shi'a doctrine of a returning figure is also traceable to Zoroastrianism (Shi'a Islam developed more in Persian regions). Other aspects of God can be incarnated in human beings, known as five 'superior ministers', and are represented by a multi-coloured five-pointed star. Most unusually for the three major monotheistic religions, they believe in reincarnation—that eventually after many lifetimes the soul will unite with the 'Cosmic Mind', and their beliefs show similarities with Gnostic beliefs. Like the Nizari Ismailis, they teach that the Koran, though sacred, is only the outer shell holding an inner esoteric meaning. They do not practise the usual Islamic customs of praying five times a day or in mosques, fasting during Ramadan and going on pilgrimage to Mecca. Often they are not regarded as being Muslim at all, nor do all the Druze consider themselves as Muslim. In fact it is sometimes suggested that they are a Christian offshoot instead. An elite of religiously trained leaders, the *uqqal*, take care of a particular region. They attend religious meetings on Thursdays at night and it requires a secret rite of induction to take part. Women can join the *uqqal* and indeed are considered better 'spiritually prepared' though they may sit separately from the men. No conversion is allowed, either in or out of the religion.

A major group of Druze is concentrated around the base of Mount Hermon in Lebanon (as mentioned in Psalm 133). Their concept of *tajalli* or *theophany* echoes the Kabbalistic teaching of the *Zohar*. The divine light of God is manifested in the material realm like a mirror image, and God interacts with the world through emanations—cf. the Tree of the Sephiroth and Gnosticism. 'Adam' has more in common with the 'original man' of the Manichaeans and of 'Adam Kadmon' of the Kabbalah. Their understanding of Jesus, too, is closer to the Docetist belief that he did not die on the cross. The four Gospels are 'holy books' and, next to Jesus, John the Baptist (*Yahya*) is revered, showing similarity with the Mandaeans. Philip Hitti mentions possible Manichaean, Mandaean and also Far Eastern influences on the beliefs. The importance of the number five, as in the five principles or 'superior ministers', especially offers Manichaean comparisons. But it is claimed that until the eighteenth century no European scholar had been allowed to see their 45 sacred books. It is sometimes said that during the Middle Ages the Druze leader Fakr ud-Din Maan II fled the Levant and tried to enlist Frankish sympathies, thus giving rise to suggestions of a connection to the Templars and to later Scottish Freemasonry, and also to the Rosicrucians. Given that Christian Rosenkreutz spent many years in the Middle East, a claim of cross-fertilization is not impossible. Owing to the strict secrecy of the Druze, however, it is difficult to see if there could have been any regular shared religious activity with the Templars, but the notion of certain ideas and practices may nonetheless have filtered through.

We might mention smaller interesting offshoots of Islam showing similar influences, such as the Sabians (distinct from the ancient Sabeans of Sheba), and the Christian Maronites of Lebanon who are also a group which came into contact with the crusaders. Although considered slightly heretical at that time, they do not appear to have strongly Gnostic or Manichaean beliefs, and therefore, though assisting the crusaders, are not necessarily relevant to the spiritual beliefs of the Templars.

The strongest influence on the Templars outside of Christianity would seem to be the Kabbalah. It is possible that in the Middle East small groups from the belief systems mentioned did meet together for mutual instruction, but the most likely influence on the Order apart from this probably came from within Christianity—the various 'heretical' sects, especially those with Docetist beliefs. Gnostic and Manichaean cosmology, like the Kabbalah, teaches a much truer picture of creation and evolution (albeit in symbolic and mythical language) than the oversimplified biblical one, which Catholic Christianity continued to teach. The problem for the Church was that people might lose the sense of importance of the physical world and especially the significance of the Resurrection, if Christ's embodiment in a human being and subsequent passing through death were denied or doubted. Templar leaders may have introduced 'denying the cross' in order that its true significance would be understood later, but maybe some brothers failed to grasp this and were genuinely led into doubt and confusion—enflamed of course by the adversary powers. Murmurings against the Order had begun before the arrests and trials; but by and large we are still left with some of the uncertainty and speculation with which this section began, except that it is hoped that the exposition on Baphomet and the 'head' with relation to the *Zohar* has brought some clarity and understanding to at least part of the allegations.

It is not the purpose of this account to dwell on any future development of Templar ideals and goals in detail (the interested individual must ponder these for him/herself) beyond the more general ideals of community and brotherhood referred to when discussing the influence of John the Baptist and of the Holy Grail (ultimately the Mani influence), which together with the transmutation of Templar wisdom by Christian Rosenkreutz (John the Evangelist) into Rosicrucianism are the threefold interweaving of the strongest influences and which overlap and mutually fertilize one another. Under the influence of John the Baptist, community and brotherhood ideals are prepared for the next epoch. Under Mani's influence, the Grail is seen as an inner path for uniting with Christ in the heart and understanding how working with the etheric—the life forces—may be developed in the future, especially in relation to transforming evil. Through Christian Rosenkreutz the transmutation into Rosicrucianism, for instance in the fields of sacred architecture and geometry, both supposedly stemming from Templar knowledge, and of healing, farming, land management and ethical economic activities come together—a uniting of science, art and religion—which leads on to spiritual science today.

Notes

1. Rudolf Steiner, *The Knights Templar. The Mystery of the Warrior Monks* (various GA) (Forest Row: Rudolf Steiner Press, 2007).
2. Dornach, 2 October 1916, GA 171, see note 1.
3. Dornach, 25 September 1916, GA 171, see note 1.
4. Basel, 19 September 1906, *The Christian Mystery*, GA 97, tr. A.R. Meuss (Gympie: Completion Press, 2000).
5. James Wasserman, *The Templars and the Assassins* (Vermont: Inner Traditions, 2001).
6. Dornach, 12 September 1924, GA 346, see note 1.
7. These streams refer to the apostles Peter and John, the former being regarded as the founder of the Christian church, originally centred in Rome, the latter as the inspirer of the more hidden 'esoteric' Christian stream.
8. Lynn Picknett and Clive Prince, *The Templar Revelation* (Bantam, Corgi Books, 1998).
9. Luke 1:17; John 1:21.
10. Dornach, 28 September 1924, *Karmic Relationships*, Vol. 4, GA 238 (Rudolf Steiner Press, 1997 ed.). Also *The Last Address* (Rudolf Steiner Press, 1967).
11. Berlin, 22 May 1905, 'The Lost Temple', from *The Temple Legend*, GA 93 (Rudolf Steiner Press, 1997).
12. Undated, 1904, see note 1.
13. Post-Atlantean epochs are time periods dated by Steiner from the destruction of Atlantis. The cultural ages are the flowering of a particular culture during these periods and denote stages of evolutionary consciousness. The dates therefore do not coincide. See Robert Powell, *Hermetic Astrology*, Vol. 1, Chapter 3 (Kinsau: Hermetika Verlag, 1987) for a fuller explanation.
14. Essenes were an esoteric Jewish sect around the time of Christ. See for example, Berne, 6 September 1910, *The Gospel of St Matthew*, GA 123 (Rudolf Steiner Press, 1965). The Dead Sea scrolls from Qumran are now known to have belonged to them.
15. Andrew Welburn, *Gnosis, the Mysteries and Christianity* (Edinburgh: Floris Books, 1994).
16. Rupert Gleadow, *The Origin of the Zodiac* (New York: Castle Books, 1968).

17. Hanover, 18 December 1910, *Background to the Gospel of St Mark*, GA 124 (Rudolf Steiner Press, 1985).

18. Sergei O. Prokofieff, *Eternal Individuality* (Temple Lodge, 1992).

19. According to spiritual science the moon sphere is not the actual moon, but a region marked by the orbit of the moon.

20. Christiania (Oslo), 17 June 1910, *The Mission of the Individual Folk Souls*, GA 121 (Rudolf Steiner Press, 1970).

21. See note 17.

22. Ibid.

23. Rudolf Steiner, *Christianity as Mystical Fact and the Mysteries of Antiquity*, GA 8, tr. A. Welburn, (AP/SteinerBooks, 2006).

24. See note 10.

25. Hella Wiesberger in *Concerning the History and Contents of the Higher Degrees of the Esoteric School 1904–1914/Freemasonry and Ritual Work*, GA 265 (Etheric Dimensions Press, 2005/ SteinerBooks 2007); Sergei O. Prokofieff, *The Mystery of John the Baptist and John the Evangelist at the Turning Point of Time*, tr. S. Blaxland-de Lange (Temple Lodge, 2005); Karl König, *The Mystery of John* (TWT Publs: Camphill Books, 2000; Edward Reaugh Smith, *The Disciple whom Jesus Loved* (Anthroposophic Press, 2000); Robert Powell, *The Mystery, Biography and Destiny of Mary Magdalene*, Chapter 3 (Lindisfarne Books, 2008).

26. Rudolf Steiner, *Esoteric Christianity*, GA 130 (Rudolf Steiner Press, 2000).

27. *From the History and Contents of the First Section of the Esoteric School 1904–1914*, GA 264, tr. J. Wood, (Hudson: Anthroposophic Press, 1998).

28. See *Concerning the History...* See note 25.

29. Virginia Sease and Manfred Schmidt-Brabant, *Paths of the Christian Mysteries*, Lecture 1, tr. M. & D. Miller. (Temple Lodge, 2003).

30. Unpublished lecture by Adriana Koulias, *Manichaeism, Catharism and Freemasonry*, Sydney 2003, www.eleggua.com

31. See *Concerning the History...* See note 25, p. 455.

32. The 'Barr' document in *Correspondence and Documents 1901–1925*, GA 262 (Rudolf Steiner Press/Anthroposophic Press, 1988), and in private reports.

33. Berlin, 6 May 1909, GA 57, *Anthroposophical Quarterly*, Vol. 9

No. 1. Conrad Fleck, *Flos and Blankflos* (New York: St George Pubns, 1977); W.J. Stein, *The Ninth Century*, Chapter 3 (Temple Lodge, 1991).

34. Ibid.
35. Paul Allen (ed.), *A Christian Rosenkreutz Anthology* (Lindisfarne Books, 2007).
36. See *The Gospel of St Matthew*, GA 123 (London: Rudolf Steiner Press, 1965); *The Gospel of St Luke*, GA 114 (Rudolf Steiner Press, 1975); *The Spiritual Guidance of the Individual and of Humanity*, GA 15 (New York: Anthroposophic Press, 1992).
37. David Ovason, *The Two Children* (London: Century, 2001).
38. Lesson of Berlin 22 October 1906, *Esoteric Lessons*, Vol. 1, GA 266/1 (Great Barrington: SteinerBooks, 2007).
39. http://en.wikipedia.org/wiki/Knights_Templar_Seal
40. Lesson of Munich 1 June 1907, *From the History and Contents...* See note 27.
41. *From the History and Contents...* See note 27, pp. 225–6.
42. Lesson of Cologne 12 February 1906, *Esoteric Lessons*, Vol. 1.
43. Düsseldorf, 5 May 1912, *The Festivals and their Meaning: Easter* (GA 130) (London: Rudolf Steiner Press, 1996).
44. Anastasius Grün (Anton Graf von Auersperg, 1806–76), *Five Easters*, tr. Charles Timothy Brooks, *German Poetry* (Boston 1853) or www.archive.org/details/germanlyrics01grgoog
45. Cologne, 10 April 1909, GA 109/111, *The Festivals and their Meaning*.
46. Berlin, 25 October 1906, *Supersensible Knowledge*, GA 55 (Rudolf Steiner Press/Anthroposophic Press, 1987).
47. Basel, 20 September 1909, *The Gospel of St Luke*, GA 114 (Rudolf Steiner Press, 1988).
48. Basel, 1 October 1911, GA 130, *Etherization of the Blood/ Reappearance of Christ in the Etheric* (SteinerBooks, 2003).
49. Dornach, 2 October 1916, GA 171, *The Knights Templar*.
50. Undated, Berlin 1904, *Gäa Sophia*, Vol. III. *The Knights Templar*.
51. *The Bridge over the River*, tr. Joseph Wetzl (Anthroposophic Press, 1974).
52. Dornach, 23 July 1922, GA 214, *The Mystery of the Trinity* (Anthroposophic Press, 1991).
53. See note 29, p. 142.

54. W.J. Stein, *The Ninth Century* (Temple Lodge, 2009).
55. Henry and Renée Kahane, *The Krater and the Grail* (University of Illinois Press, 1965).
56. Lynn Picknett and Clive Prince, *The Sion Revelation* (New York: Touchstone, 2006).
57. Landin, 29 July 1906, *The Christian Mystery*, GA 97 (Gympie: Completion Press, 2000).
58. Berlin, 28 March 1905, GA 92, Typescript NSL 175–6.
59. Dornach, 16 April 1921, *Materialism and the Task of Anthroposophy*, GA 204 (Rudolf Steiner Press/Anthroposophic Press, 1987).
60. By Judith von Halle at the Templar Conferences of 2007 and 2009, Hamburg and Forest Row.
61. Translated by P.M. Matarasso (Penguin Books, 1975).
62. *The Sovereign Adventure: The Grail of Mankind* (James Clarke & Co. Ltd., 1971).
63. Dornach, 25 September 1916, GA 171, *The Knights Templar*.
64. Berlin, 11 November 1904, *The Temple Legend*, GA 93, tr. J.M. Wood (Rudolf Steiner Press, 1997).
65. Richard Seddon, *Mani* (Temple Lodge, 1998); Kurt Rudolph, *Gnosis* (T. & T. Clarke Ltd., 1983).
66. *The Apocalypse of St John*, GA 104 (London: Rudolf Steiner Press, 1977).
67. Esoteric Lesson 1911, in *From the History and Contents* ... see note 27, p. 215.
68. See note 2.
69. Guenther Wachsmuth, *The Face of the Earth and the Destiny of Mankind*, lecture given at Dornach 27 December 1923, quoted in Sylvia Francke and Thomas Cawthorne, *The Tree of Life and the Holy Grail* (Temple Lodge, 1996).
70. Dornach, 12 September 1924, *The Knights Templar*, see note 1; also *The Book of Revelation*, GA 346 (London: Rudolf Steiner Press. 1998).
71. Steven Runciman, *The Medieval Manichee* (Cambridge University Press, 1984).
72. See the chapter 'The "Secret Statutes"'.
73. Iain Gardner and S.N.E. Lieu (eds.), *Manichaean Texts from the Roman Empire*, p. 242 (Cambridge University Press, 2004).
74. *Concerning the History and Contents* ... see note 25, p. 115.

75. See note 56.
76. *The Element Encyclopaedia of Secret Societies and Hidden History* (London: HarperElement, 2006).
77. See note 56.
78. Morton Smith, *The Secret Gospel* (California: Dawn Horse Press, 1982).
79. Andrew Welburn, *Gnosis* (Edinburgh: Floris Books, 1994).
80. Isabel Cooper-Oakley, *Masonry and Medieval Mysticism* (Theosophical Publishing House, 1977).
81. Aimée Bothwell-Gosse,*The Knights Templars* (Office of the Co-Mason, n.d.).
82. T.H. Meyer, *D.N. Dunlop* (Temple Lodge, 1992).
83. Steiner spoke of three principal adversary powers: Lucifer, who would entice people away from the earth into an illusory state; Ahriman, who wishes to harden and materialize everything connected to the earth; Sorat, the Sun-demon who opposes Christ and, together with the Asuras, attacks the human ego or spiritual individuality.
84. Dornach, 12 September 1924 , see note 70.
85. Dornach, 25 September 1916, *The Knights Templar* (see note 1); also *Inner Impulses of Evolution*, GA 171 (New York: Anthroposophic Press, 1984).
86. Berlin, 22 May 1905, *The Knights Templar*; also *The Temple Legend*, GA 93 (Rudolf Steiner Press, 1997).
87. M. Michelet, *Le Procès des Templiers, Tome II*, p. 400 (Paris 1851).
88. Malcolm Barber, *The Trial of the Templars* (Folio Society, 2003).
89. See note 86.
90. Dornach, 2 October 1916, *The Knights Templar*.
91. Carlo Pietzner, *Of the Templar Impulse in Our Time,* lecture, Copake, New York, 31 December 1966, private printing.
92. See note 88.
93. See note 88.
94. René Gilles, *Les Templiers—sont ils coupables?* (Paris: Henri Guichaou, 1957). Gérard de Serbanesco, *Histoire de l'Ordre des Templiers et les Croisades* (Paris: Les Editions Byblos, 1969). Translations are from Serbanesco's version by M.J.
95. M. Michelet, *Le Procès des Templiers, Tome I*, p. 88.
96. Gian Domenico Mansi, 1692–1769, Italian theologian and his-

torian, best known for his 31 volume edition of the Councils, *Sacrorum Conciliorum nova et amplissimo collectio* (1758–98). Prutz quotes from Vol. 19.

97. Thomas Parker, *The Knights Templar in England* (University of Arizona Press, 1963).

98. Details of Roncelin de Fos are taken from two articles by Jean-Pierre Schmit and Jean de Lauris in *Le Médiéviste Magazine*, Nr. 15 (Figeac, n.d.), no longer published.

99. See note 71.

100. See note 98.

101. Julius Evola, *The Mystery of the Grail* (Vermont: Inner Traditions, 1997).

102. The Chinon Parchment, released from the Vatican in 2007. For a translation, see http://asv.vatican.va/en/doc/1308.htm

103. See note 87.

104. Laurent Dailliez, *Les Templiers en Provence* (Nice: Alpes-Méditerranée-Éditions, 1977). He states that Roncelin was Master in England as early as 1236, and visitor in Italy from 1263 to 1265. Dailliez in *Les Templiers, Gouvernement et Institutions, Tome 1* (Nice 1980) incidentally lists some chaplains presented to local bishops for ordination by Masters in England— both Robert de Sandfort and Roncelin de Fos are listed as Masters.

105. See note 5.

106. See note 88.

107. E.G. Léonard, *Introduction au Cartulaire Manuscrit du Temple 1150–1317* (Paris 1930).

108. See note 39.

109. Malcolm Barber, *The Trial of the Templars*, see note 88.

110. From www.veling.nl/anne/templars/mysteries.html

111. See note 108.

112. Ibid.

113. Charles G. Addison, *The History of the Knights Templars*, p. 256 (Black Books, 1995).

114. See note 108.

115. Berlin, 22 May 1905, *The Knights Templar*, also *The Temple Legend*, GA 93.

116. *How to Know Higher Worlds*, GA 10, Chapter 10: paragraph 4, 6, 12 (Anthroposophic Press, 1994).

117. *The Way of Self Knowledge and the Threshold of the Spiritual World*, GA 16, 17, p. 46 (SteinerBooks, 2006).

118. *How to Know Higher Worlds*, Chapter 11: paragraph nos. 9, 11.

119. See note 91.

120. Landin, 29 July 1906, *The Christian Mystery*, GA 97 (Gympie: Completion Press, 2000).

120a. We might add here that in the mid-thirteenth century for a short time there was apparently a 'spiritual eclipse', and even highly developed people could no longer see into the spiritual world. It was thus easier for distortions to arise. Neuchâtel, 27 September 1911, *Esoteric Christianity*, GA 130 (Rudolf Steiner Press, 2000).

121. www.the-orb.net/encyclop/religion/monastic/ricaut.html

122. http://templarresearch.1.makeforum.org/2008/10/28/who-was-bafometz/

123. Hugh Schonfield, *The Essene Odyssey* (Element Books, 1993).

124. Eliphas Lévi, *Transcendental Magic*, tr. A.E. Waite (London: Rider, 1984).

125. Idries Shah, *The Sufis* (New York: Doubleday, 1964).

126. *Faculty Meetings With Rudolf Steiner*, Vol. 1, Wednesday, 9 June 1920 (Anthroposophic Press, 1998).

127. Vienna, 13 April 1914, *The Inner Nature of Man*, GA 153, tr. A.R. Meuss (Rudolf Steiner Press, 1994).

128. Malcolm Barber, see note 88.

129. Juliet Faith, *The Knights Templar in Somerset* (Stroud: The History Press, 2009).

130. Emil Bock, *Genesis*, p. 153 (Edinburgh: Floris Books, 1983).

131. *The High Book of the Grail (Perlevaus)*, p. 35, tr. Nigel Bryant (Cambridge: D.S. Brewer, 1978).

132. Ibid., p. 73.

133. See note 110.

134. Sergei O. Prokofieff, *The Spiritual Origins of Eastern Europe and the Future Mystery of the Holy Grail*, Chapter 3 (Temple Lodge, 1993).

135. See Patrice Chaplain, *City of Secrets* (London: Constable & Robinson, 2007), for interesting references to the history of the Kabbalah in Girona and the new Kabbalah Centre.

136. J.M. Upton-Ward, *The Rule of the Templars*, Article 678 (Woodbridge: Boydell Press, 1992).

137. Eliphas Lévi, *The Book of Splendours* (Wellingborough: Aquarian Press, 1983).
138. *The Kabbalah Unveiled*, tr. S.L. MacGregor Mathers from the *Kabbala Denudata* (London: Routledge & Kegan Paul, 1981).
139. Basel, 20 September 1909, *The Gospel of St Luke*, GA 114 (Rudolf Steiner Press, 1975).
140. Emil Bock, *The Childhood of Jesus*, Chapter 1 (Edinburgh: Floris Books, 1997).
141. Compiled from James Wasserman, *The Templars and the Assassins* (Vermont: Inner Traditions, 2001), and Arkon Daraul, *Secret Societies* (London: Tandem Books, 1965).
142. See note 125.
143. Dornach, 8 August 1924, *Karmic Relationships*, Vol. 3, GA 237, tr. G. Adams & D.S. Osmond (Rudolf Steiner Press, 1977).
144. See Philip K. Hitti, *Origins of the Druze, People and Religion* (1924).

Index of Names and Places

As surnames only gradually came into use during the Middle Ages, all names of that period are listed under the first name